The Ask Us Anything
(About the Quad-Cities)
Book

By the staff of Quad-Cities Online®
Copyright 2004, Moline Dispatch Publishing Co. L.L.C.
All rights reserved. No part of this publication may be reproduced,
transmitted, transcribed or translated by any means
without the prior written consent of
Moline Dispatch Publishing Co.
1720 5th Ave.
Moline, IL 61265

Printed by
Brandt Co.
3020 Hickory Grove Road
Davenport, IA 52806

ISBN 0-9761162-0-0

The Introduction

In 1998, Quad-Cities Online® launched a new feature called "Ask Us Anything (About the Quad-Cities)." It was an immediate hit. The questions poured in; thousands of people faithfully read the question of the day and clicked on the "answer" button; other media outlets began copy-cat features.

Many of the questions sent "Ask Us Anything" are topical. People want to know, for example, what workers are doing on a bridge, or why a street is torn up, or what business will be in the new building under contruction.

A good many questions, though, are "evergreens" — the answers will change little, if any, with the passage of time. This book is a collection of these evergreens.

We dedicate it to the Quad-Citians whose curiousity about their community has made "Ask Us Anything" enjoyable to the public, and to those of us at Quad-Cities Online® who engage in a never-ending search for answers.

How it's done

Anyone who wishes to e-mail a question, or contribute to an answer, can visit www.qconline.com and click on Ask Us Anything. Because the editors receive dozens of questions a week, but can only answer one a day, many questions must be left unanswered. We choose to answer questions that we believe will interest the most readers, or are timely, or particularly interesting.

For answers, we turn to various sources: the archives and staff of The Dispatch and The Rock Island Argus; local experts on certain topics; libraries; and of course, the Internet.

Our best source often turns out to be the Ask Us readers and their web of friends and colleagues who love the hunt for information as much as we do! Thanks to all of you.

Table of Contents

The Name Game

Q: What was the first city in the Quad-Cities? Where did the names come from?

A: The first of the current names to appear was Davenport, which was platted and named May 14, 1836. It's named for Col. George Davenport, the first permanent white settler in the area.

Rock Island, though, is the first when predecessor names are considered.

Rock Island was formed in 1841 from Farnhamsburg and Stephenson, both named after early settlers. Farnhamsburg was in existence by 1833, when it was designated the seat of newly formed Rock Island County. The plat for Stephenson was filed on July 10, 1835. Stephenson's name was changed to Rock Island in 1841 and the city expanded to include Farnhamsburg. The name, Rock Island, was of course taken from the nearby island in the Mississippi.

An interesting account of how Stephenson came to be Stephenson rather than Davenport, the name preferred by its founders, can be found in H. E. Downer's 1910 "History of Davenport and Scott County," Chapter 31. It's available on the Web at http://www.celticcousins.net/scott/chapter31.html.

Among the other Quad-Cities, Moline is next oldest. It was platted in 1843. Its name is based on "moulin," the French word for "mill."

Without taking sides in the argument over whether East Moline or Bettendorf is the fourth "Quad-City":

East Moline was incorporated in 1903. Among its constituent parts is Watertown, a village platted in 1857.

Bettendorf has been Bettendorf since 1903, when Gilbertown (founded 1858) changed its name to honor William and Joseph Bettendorf, brothers who'd agreed to move their iron-wagon business to the village.

Q: Was Silvis once named Pleasant Valley?

A: Yes. The area incorporated as the village of Silvis in 1906 was for at least 50 years known as Pleasant Valley. The village took its name from Richard Shippen Silvis, an early settler who, with his brother, operated the Silvis Mining Co.

Richard Shippen Silvis (1839-1918). The village of Silvis is named for this early settler. (Photo / Silvis family Web site)

Richard Shippen Silvis arrived in Pleasant Valley in 1854, when he was 14 or 15 years old, according to a family account on this Web site: http://homepages.rootsweb.com/~marier/Stories-Pics/683.htm~.

It says, "In 1853, Grandpa Silvis (#223 John) left Jefferson County, Pennsylvania, with some of his family members and headed for Rock Island County, Illinois. They arrived there in 1854 and settled in a small area called Pleasant Valley in Hampton Twp. Pleasant Valley was a small community of farmers and coal miners and was on the stage line that ran from Rock Island to Chicago. Later the Chicago and Rock Island Railroad ran through the farm land of this community.

"It was in 1905 that the name of Pleasant Valley was changed to 'Silvis' in honor of #686, Richard Shippen Silvis, or Uncle Ship.

"In Pleasant Valley, Uncle Ship and Uncle Sharp owned and operated the Silvis Mining Company. They were both highly respected men in their community and both held offices of trust and honor. Uncle Ship's obituary states that he was active in politics and he held office as Road Commissioner and was School Director for many years. Uncle Sharp served his community as Commissioner of Highways, Township Collector, Town Supervisor, member of the School District, and Sheriff. Both brothers were Democrats and members of the Methodist Church."

An extensive history of the Silvis family in America can be found at this site: http://homepages.rootsweb. com/marier/Index.htm.

Q: When did Milan's name change from Camden Mills, and why?

A: To begin at the beginning ...

A man named William Dickson laid out the village in 1843 and — for reasons we don't know —named it Camden. In 1848, "Mills" was added to the name and it became Camden Mills. The change was said to have occurred because there was another "Camden" in Illinois, in Schuyler County. "Mills" was picked as an addition to Camden's name because a flour mill and sawmill were major industries at the time.

The name was changed to Milan in 1870. Though we've seen no well-sourced accounts of why the name changed, a popular story has it that village fathers were attempting to lure a watch manufacturer to town and changed the name to Milan since it had a "European" flavor and the legend "Made in Milan" might spur watch sales.

Alas, the story goes, while the watchmaker did build a factory in Milan, the equipment proved unworkable and no watches were made.

Q: I live in Orion and was wondering where Orion got its name from.

A: According to a history of Orion on the Orion Chamber of Commerce Web site, the town now known as Orion was platted by Charles Wesley Dean in 1853 and named Deanington. (Earlier, there are references to a colony called LaGrange, also. The first settlers arrived in the late 1830s.)

The name was changed to "Orion" November 11, 1865, to match the name of a nearby post office that had been established in 1848 and named Orion, after the constellation, by Charles Trego, the first postmaster.

No word on when the pronunciation changed from "o-RYE-un" to "OR-ee-un."

Q: How many different names has the baseball team now known as the Swing had?

A: We don't have a definitive answer for you, but can say that

"Swing of the Quad-Cities" is at least the ninth name for a professional baseball team based in Davenport.

Minor League Baseball's official Web site says professional baseball arrived in Davenport in 1888, when the city had teams in two leagues. The name of one, an entry in the short-lived Central Interstate League, apparently is lost, but the second team, a member of the Western Association, was known as the Onion Weeders. We assume the name was a reference to the vast onion fields in the area at the time.

Subsequent Davenport teams were known as the River Rats, the Prodigals and the Blue Sox, as the team was named in 1914. The minorleagebaseball.com article primarily is about the 1933 Blue Sox, which the site lists as the 58th best minor-league team of all time.

The Blue Sox had a long run, and we're unsure whether a different name was used before the Davenport team entered the Midwest League in 1960 as the Braves. Here's a list of names from 1960 onward:

- *Davenport Braves, 1960*
- *Quad Cities Braves, 1961*
- *Quad Cities Angels, 1962-76*
- *Quad City Angels, 1977-78*
- *Quad City Cubs, 1979-84*
- *Quad City Angels, 1985-91*
- *Quad City River Bandits, 1992-2003*
- *Swing of the Quad Cities, 2004-??*

Perhaps some of our readers will be able to fill in any names we've missed.

A reader adds: In the late '40s, the Davenport Class B minor league baseball team was known as the Quad-City Quads. I still have a seat cushion that reads "Property of Quad-City Quads To Be Rented Not Sold." Before that, in the early to mid '40s, Moline had a team in the Three-I League, named the Moline Athletics.

Another reader adds: Before the Quad-City Quads, there was a team called the Davenport Pirates. Probably around 1945 or 1946.

And yet another: "In the late 40's/early 50's we were the Davenport Tigers, Davenport Pirates, Quad-City Quads, Dav-Sox (a White Sox farm team)."

And one more: "I was a ball shagger for the Moline Three I team in the late 1930's — the team was called the Moline Plowboys; players such as Kirby Higbee, Eddie Waitkus, Mizell Platt, Swish Nicholson, Mike Gazella (Mgr — who brought in Babe Ruth for a hitting exposition; he promptly hit a few over the right field Fieldhouse)."

Q: When I was a kid, back in the 1930s, there was an office building at the corner of 18th Street & 3rd Avenue in Rock Island. It was called the "Safety Building." How did it get this name?

A: First, the Safety Building is still at the corner of 18th Street and 3rd Avenue, and it is still called the Safety Building.

Its name apparently is based on the construction materials. When it was built in 1907-08, reinforced concrete was used for what was said to be the first time in the Quad-Cities. It was termed "fireproof" by an insurance rating company. For more about the past, present and future of the Safety Building, visit this Web site: http://www.iltrails.org/rockisland/ripscards/safetybldg.html.

Q: **Where did the sports field for United Township High School get its name?**

A: The Soule Bowl commemorates Dr. A. E. Soule, the first chairman of the East Moline Park Board and the man whose idea it was to build a stadium in the natural bowl in the Butterworth Park hillside. He then oversaw planning and construction.

Constructed under the auspices of the Works Progress Administration, Soule Bowl hosted its first game Oct. 17, 1936. Kewanee won, 7-6, over what was then the East Moline High School Hilltoppers. The first home win came a week later, 39-0, over St. Joseph's of Rock Island.

Dr. A. E. Soule

Dr. Soule, active in civic affairs throughout his life, died Aug. 12, 1949, at age 72.

Q: **I now live out of state but grew up near Fejervary Park. A large part of my childhood was spent in this park. What are its origins? Where did it get its name? When was it founded?**

A: The story of Fejervary Park begins with Count Nicholas Fejervary, who was born in Hungary in 1811. As a young man, his political views got him into trouble. He was either sent, or voluntarily went, into exile, and ended up in Davenport sometime prior to 1850.

He acquired various properties in and around the city, and these passed to his daughter Celestine when he died in 1895.

In 1902, Celestine donated 21 acres to Davenport. In 1903, the city's park commission purchased an adjoining 19 acres from F. H. Griggs for $7,500. The area was a park from that point on, though various of its zoo-like features were added piecemeal over the years.

A signature attraction, Monkey Island, opened in 1927 or 1928 and drew visitors until 2000, when the monkeys were removed to a new home in Texas as part of a revamp that turned the park's focus to animals native to the Midwest.

Q: **Who, what, when and why did the name "Avenue of the Cities" come into existence?**

A: The first reference to "Avenue of the Cities" in our files came in an Oct. 28, 1993, news story, which reported that a business group called Friends of the Avenue wanted the name changed on the street that had one end in Moline (23rd Avenue), continued through East Moline (42nd Avenue) and had the other end in Colona (Colona Avenue).

The goal, the group said, was "to revitalize the aging retail strip (without stopping) at any city borders."

"Right now, it has three names. It's called 23rd, 42nd and Colona avenue. That can be pretty confusing for people getting off the interstate. Instead, we want one name," the group's spokesperson said then.

It took nearly nine years and commitments from Moline, East Moline, Silvis, Colona and the Illinois

Department of Transportation, but the name change finally became official Sept. 30, 2002, when new signs went up along the route.

Whether the name change will have the desired impact remains to be seen, and we're not sure exactly how success will be measured.

Q: Rumor has it that there used to be a large sofa/furniture manufacturing plant in Davenport. As a result, this is why people call sofas "davenports" around this area. Is this true, and when/where did the plant exist?

A: As far as we know, this is not true, although it makes sense.

Most kinds of furniture are either named for their function or their maker.

However, the origins of the use of *davenport* as a synonym for couch or sofa are murky.

For starters, in Britain a davenport is a writing desk, not a sofa. Some believe that the furniture maker Gillows of London first created this hinged-lid desk around 1790 for a Capt. John Davenport.

The earliest written reference cited for a davenport *couch* is in an 1897 article in the Washington Post, according to Take Our Word For It, which adds, "Oddly, in the earliest record of the writing desk (1853) it is spelled Devonport, like the place. (It's a port. In Devon.) Just to add to the glorious confusion, Davenport (with a capital D) is a kind of Staffordshire china which was made between 1793 and 1882 by the Davenport family of Longport."

Whew.

Also keep in mind that in much of America at one time, most people thought a davenport was a sofa-bed. Peter Kroehler of the Kroehler Co., patented the first foldout "davenport bed" with hidden mattress and springs in 1906.

All this aside, there was a furniture company with the right name at about the right time: A.H. Davenport of Boston, which was nationally known beginning in the 1880s. The founder, according to the city of Cambridge, Mass., was Albert H. Davenport, a native of Malden, Mass.

In 1880 he bought the Boston furniture company where he'd been working for 14 years. The business flourished, and though Davenport died in 1906, his business continued successfully. (It combined with a competitor, Irving & Casson in 1914. In the 1950s, Irving & Casson-A.H. Davenport completed a job of note: the interior of the United Nations building in New York. The company continued to operate until the early 1970s.)

We don't know if Mr. Davenport was especially well-known for making couches, although you can find some examples of very elegant ones made by his company at this Web site: http://www.eastman.org/3_histhse/hall.html.

Q: Who is "Lake George" in the Loud Thunder Forest Preserve named for, if anyone?

A: The 170-acre lake is named for George Strombeck, who was a member of what was then the Rock Island County Board of Supervisors when the lake was first proposed in 1959.

Mr. Strombeck, who died in 1960, was praised as the "prime mover" in the project when the dam that created the lake was dedicated in 1966.

^{The}Name Game

Q: Who was Fred Schwengel? There is a sign on the I-80 bridge heading into Illinois that says the bridge was named for him?

A: Fred Schwengel (1903-1993) served a total of eight terms in the U.S. House of Representatives, where, as a member of the Public Works Committee, he was among the key movers in the creation of the interstate highway system.

A native of Sheffield, Iowa, he moved to Davenport after graduating from college. A Republican, he represented Scott County in the Iowa Legislature from 1944 to 1954. He was elected to Congress in 1954 and served until 1964, when he lost his seat in the Lyndon Johnson landslide over Barry Goldwater in that year's presidential election. He won his seat back in 1966 and served until 1972, when he retired from politics after being defeated again.

An amateur historian, he was a noted Lincoln scholar and was instrumental in forming the U. S. Capitol Historical Society.

There's a brief biography of Mr. Schwengel at this Web page: http://bioguide.congress.gov/scripts/biodisplay.pl?index=S000161.

Q: Who is Wharton Field House in Moline named after? How about Browning Field?

A: Wharton Field House is named after T. F. Wharton.

Mr. Wharton was president of the Maroon and White Association in 1928, the year the the fieldhouse was constructed. It was known as the Moline Field House until 1941, when a petition drive requesting it be named after Mr. Wharton was conducted.

Mr. Wharton, a longtime employee of Deere & Co. who was secretary-treasurer of the firm when he retired, died in 1943.

Browning Field is named after John T. Browning, who made a death-bed change in his will in 1910 to leave the land to the city of Moline for use as an athletic field. Mr. Browning, an attorney, was the first president of the Moline Library Board and helped acquire land for and build the downtown library.

Q: Who was George Thuenen, for whom the bridge/road into the Isle of Capri boat is named? What is/was his significance to get a road named for him?

A: Mr. Thuenen, who died in 1997 at the age of 93, was a former mayor of Bettendorf and a former chairman of the Scott County Board.

Following is information about him excerpted from a series of stories published in observance of Bettendorf's centennial:

"The fifth in the series of Progressive Party mayors, George R. Thuenen (mayor 1962-1968), was born on a farm on Middle Road on Aug. 25, 1904. He had nine siblings, and at the age of 8 delivered milk with a horse and wagon to Davenport's McClellan Heights neighborhood. He rode a horse to Sudlow School for eighth and ninth grades, but did not attend high school.

"Thuenen joined the Navy in 1927 and saw the Panama Canal aboard the USS Idaho. He was honorably discharged in 1931. He married Ruth Incze on April 23, 1932, and ran

The Name Game

Thuenen's Shell Service Station in Bettendorf from 1937 to 1969.

"Before he was elected mayor, he served on the Bettendorf School Board from 1949 to 1955. He helped plan Bettendorf High School and Jefferson, Jackson, Grant Wood and Mark Twain elementary schools.

"He was a charter member of the Bettendorf Chamber of Commerce and served as its president in 1957-58. He also was a charter member of the Bettendorf Lions Club and the Rotary. While mayor, he was chairman of the Quad-City Conference of Mayors.

"After he stepped down as mayor, he served on the Scott County Board of Supervisors from 1968 to 1978. In 1983 he was appointed a commissioner of the Scott County Landfill. His son, George Thuenen IV, sat on the Bettendorf City Council from 1978 to 1986."

A reader adds: Mr. Thuenen also was a charter member of Hamilton Lodge No. 665 and served as master of the lodge in 1960, He was buried with full Masonic honors.

Q: Who was John O'Donnell?

A: Mr. O'Donnell was a long-time sports editor of the Davenport Times-Democrat.

What was then Davenport Municipal Stadium was renamed May 27, 1971, to honor him.

The stadium was built in 1931. How long it remains John O'Donnell Stadium is an open question as of this writing (summer 2004). The city and the Swing of the Quad-Cities, the current professional baseball team, are attempting to sell naming rights to John O'Donnell, which underwent a $13.5 million revamp in 2003-04.

Q: How did Devil's Glen Park get its name? Did something horrible happen in that little valley of Duck Creek many years ago that led to such a fiendish name?

A: That sounds like two questions, and we'll take a shot at both.

1. A couple of years ago, The Dispatch and Argus Life Department did a Halloween trivia contest in which the park name question was asked. The answer:

"The story goes that a Native American who once lived in a cave in the area was called a 'devil' by the nearby ethnocentric white settlers. (It is unknown if said 'devil' ever caused anyone any harm.) At some point the area became known as Devil's Glen — a name later attached to the park and, later yet, to the road."

We weren't entirely satisfied with this explanation, so we asked around.

One astute suggestion was that limestone formations frequently are called the Devil's Punchbowl, etc. (There's one of those at Wildcat Den State Park near Muscatine.)

Though the Indian story is possible, and has been cited by amateur historians, it's also possible that the name also has something to do with the reaction of somebody's colorful imagination to the rock formations along the creek.

2. The park has been the site of at least one horrible happening. On March 5, 1988, the body of Joseph Brown was discovered in a ravine in the park. Mr. Brown, 30, had been shot twice in the head with a .22-caliber handgun. Paul A. Anderson was convicted of Mr. Brown's murder. Mr. Anderson and Mr. Brown met while they were inmates in the East Moline Correctional Center and had been part of the same burglary ring. At trial, prosecutors argued that Mr. Anderson believed Mr. Brown had cheated him out of his share of the ring's proceeds.

Mr. Brown's wife, Laura, was found murdered on the same day as her husband.

She was stabbed 27 times in their Moline home. No one was ever charged with her murder.

Q: Who is Stephens Park in Moline named after?

A: The park is named after the family of Moline industrialist George W. Stephens (1799-1892), who arrived here in 1841. He worked in the agriculture industry, affiliated with Candee, Swan & Co. in 1868, becoming its president when it was later reorganized as the Moline Plow Co. The company eventually owned 21 buildings along 3rd Avenue in Moline.

His son, George Arthur Stephens, also was president of Moline Plow Co.

According to a May 6, 1972, story written by longtime Dispatch librarian Evy Thompson, Moline acquired a small parcel of land in what eventually became Stephens Park in 1907. In 1912, George A. Stephens donated a "large" amount of adjacent land to the city. In 1915-16, the city acquired small holdings from three additional families to round out the park to its present 19.1 acres. The

George W. Stephens

park is on the west side of 7th Street from 12th to 15th avenues.

On a somewhat related note: In 1927, Mr. Stephens' sister, Ada, donated 1.32 acres to the city for what became Stephens Square on the west side of 19th Street from 6th to 7th avenues.

In the early 1970s, there was a years-long fight to prevent part of Stephens Square from being used for the Interstate 74 exchange. Eventually, roadbuilders got strips of land on the south and east sides of the square, and the city got title to state-owned land west of the square in compensation.

Some miscellaneous items of note:

• Among other things, George W. Stephens helped David Sears build a sawmill, and organized a furniture company in the late 1850s with Sears and Jonathan Huntoon. A set of "Rock Island" chairs made by their company was donated to the Colonel Davenport Historical Foundation in 1998.

• Ada Stephens was noted as a community philanthropist. When she donated Stephens Square to the city, she stipulated that any tree removed from the park should be replaced as soon as possible. When a giant silver maple — thought to be 80-90 years old — was done in by an ice storm in 1995, the city replaced it with two sugar maples.

Q: How did Loud Thunder Forest Preserve get its name?

A: "Loud Thunder" was picked by a citizens' committee from among 337 entries submitted in a 1948 "Name That Park" contest.

The suggestion of Thomas W. Rogers of Moline, the name is the

The Name Game

English spelling of Nah-Se-Us-Kuk, the eldest son of Black Hawk, the famed Sauk war leader. The selection was made based on criteria that said the name should be associated with the area's historical significance and/or "some outstanding person." Mr. Rogers received $15 as a prize when his suggestion was adopted.

The same contest, incidentally, produced two of the other park names still in use within Rock Island County's Forest Preserve District.

"Illiniwek," the park/campground on the Mississippi near Hampton, was suggested by Katherine Walther of Port Byron and is based on the name of an important group of Illinois Indians.

"Indian Bluff," the park/golf course just south of Quad City International Airport, was suggested by Bob VanDeMaele of Rock Island, who said he picked the name because the land was once owned by Indians and that "Indians are the only true Americans."

Loud Thunder, 1,600 acres of wooded hills, was purchased by Rock Island County for $34,000 in 1944, and was known as the Searle Tract or Searle Ranch until the the 1948 naming contest. The dam that created the 167-acre Lake George was built by the county a number of years later.

Q: How did they get the name "The Mark" and what, if anything, does it stand for?

A: The full, official name "The MARK of the Quad-Cities" was selected by the civic center board in 1992 after a four-month search that included consideration of thousands of computer-generated names and payment of $8,000 to a Minneapolis consulting firm specializing in corporate identity issues.

During much of the planning and construction stages, the building was called the Quad City Civic Center, but officials thought that much too blah.

They wanted a one-word name that was easy to say and easy to remember. They believed the "Mark" fit that bill, and officials were further attracted to it because of its many definitions.

It echoes the river — it's a navigational term; it also means a "recognized standard of quality," an object or point that "serves as a guide," a "distinctive trait or quality" and something of "lasting effect," among other things.

Before making the final selection, the board tested reaction to the name among potential users, and the feedback was all positive.

There was a minor controversy at the time because of the $8,000 consulting fee and the fact that suggestions from local residents weren't solicited.

But the fussing quickly faded as the new arena rapidly established itself as one of the most successful in the country.

It still is: Some years, ticket sales for Mark events run ahead of even Chicago's United Center, home of the Bulls and an arena that seats nearly twice as many people.

Q: Who was Camp McClellan and McClellan Heights in Davenport named after?

A: Both are named after George B. McClellan, the general who commanded Union forces early in the Civil War. Dismissed by President Lincoln for inaction, later reinstated, he was again dismissed when he failed to meet Lincoln's desire that he actively engage Confederate forces.

The Democratic candidate for president against Lincoln in 1864, McClellan won only three states.

Camp McClellan was centered in what is now Lindsay Park in the Village of East Davenport. It was the major training site for new soldiers from Iowa and Illinois, and also served as a prison camp for nearly 200 Sioux Indians detained after an 1862 uprising in Minnesota.

McClellan Heights, one of Davenport's prime neighborhoods, overlooks Lindsay Park.

Davenport's Camp McClellan, incidentally, was but one of several "Camp McClellans" around the country during the Civil War.

Q: Can you tell me anything about New Windsor? Someone said there was a fire and that is why it is called "New" Windsor.

A: The first thing to know is that New Windsor, a village of 720 people in Mercer County, about 25 miles southeast of the Quad-Cities, isn't really "New" Windsor. The official name is "Village of Windsor."

The village, named after Windsor Castle in Scotland, was incorporated as Windsor on Aug. 14, 1869. The founders belatedly discovered that there already was a Windsor, Ill. — the City of Windsor, which had been incorporated Feb. 16, 1865.

To avoid confusion, both the post office and the train station in the new municipality were named "New Windsor," and the village has been called that ever since, and is marked as such on maps.

The City of Windsor, in Shelby County in central Illinois, had a population in 2000 of 1,125. It's marked on maps simply as "Windsor."

Q: I live in Florida now after growing up in Moline, and some friends and I were talking the other day about activities we did as youngsters and places that we had visited and/or camped. Could you please tell me the name of the Girl Scout Lodge that used to be (and may still be) in Black Hawk State Park? I remember staying there but can't remember the name.

A: The name that's slipped your memory is Singing Bird Lodge. The Girl Scouts returned the property to the state a number of years back, and the state deeded it to the Illinois Historic Preservation Agency. It is now the Singing Bird Nature Center and is used by Black Hawk State Historic Site as an education center.

ᴬBit of Nature

Q: **I lived in Bettendorf at one time, and it was rumored that there were water moccasin snakes in the creeks there. Is this true?**

A: Probably not, assuming people were using "water moccasin" as a synonym for "cottonmouth."

The general range of the cottonmouth, a highly poisonous pit viper, is south of a line running through far southern Missouri and Illinois. Iowa Herpetology says, "The famous, and venomous, cottonmouth (or water moccasin), Agkistrodon piscivorus, is not found in Iowa. The farthest north cottonmouths have been recorded is central Missouri."

People do tend to refer to all water snakes as water moccasins, so we wouldn't be surprised if people said they were present in the Quad-Cities area. We would be very surprised if they actually were.

A reader adds: "On the cottonmouth question: I actually caught a cottonmouth snake in Iowa while fishing at Lake Geode in West Burlington about 8 years ago. It was confirmed by a DNR ranger, so they can be found a little farther north than central Missouri as your response indicated. Luckily, it was drowned when I reeled it in and could not have bitten me. It was at least four feet in length, two inches in diameter and had very large, hinged fangs, which the ranger showed me."

Another says: "I beg to differ on your answer on the cottonmouths. You stated that the farthest north cottonmouths are found is central Missouri. I grew up in Colona, Ill., and there were always cottonmouths found in the Hennipen Canal & the backwaters of the Green River. Might want to pass this along."

And another: "On the cottonmouth question, about 30 years ago a teen-ager was bit by a cottonmouth on the Rock River near East Moline. He was rushed to the hospital, and it was confirmed he had been bitten by a poisonous snake."

And one more: "More on the Cottonmouths … I was at Catttail Slough just south of Fulton, Illinois, last week on Monday, 4/19/04, and was throwing some jigs near the boat ramp and spooked one sunning himself (herself?) in some tree roots and took off for the water and yes, I do know what a cottonmouth looks like. This one was dern near 4 ft. in length @ approx. 2 inches in diameter. Got my attention and I WENT the other way!"

This is one of a dozen large trees taken down by a tornado that touched down in Moline's Riverside Park June 20, 1974. (Photo / file)

Q: **In the 1970s a tornado crossed the river and went through the Riverside Cemetery causing some damage. What year and month was that?**

A Bit of Nature

A: That was June 20, 1974. A severe storm front moved through the Quad-Cities in the early evening, spawning high winds and several funnel clouds.

One of the funnel clouds took the roof off the Holiday Inn in Bettendorf, jumped the J.I. Case plant in Bettendorf, touched down in the Mississippi and then churned into Moline.

It snapped seven 60,000-volt power lines, cutting electricity to more than 6,000 people and setting fire to two sheds belonging to American Air Filter. It also ripped roofs off several businesses in the area and then snapped or uprooted a dozen large trees in Riverside Park before lifting. Only one injury was reported.

Moline emergency officials said at the time it was the first known tornado touchdown in the city. Until that day, local folkfore had it that the size and and configuration of the river here protected Moline from tornado touchdowns.

Q: I am working on a transcription of my great-grandfather's 5-year diary, which he (Jacob Stewart) kept as a teenager in the 1870s. The family lived in the Rock Island vicinity from 1877-81, then moved on to settle in Howard Co., Neb. While near Rock Island, Jacob wrote often about going to the Dosia, and once mentioned the mouth of the Dosia. Was this a river or stream? Did it succumb to flood control measures, no longer existing as a place name? Thank you, Dori

A: "Dosia" is a shortened version of Meredosia, which is a corruption of the French "mer d' osier" or "sea of willows."

The Meredosia is the area of a prehistoric bed of the Mississippi River roughly between the towns of Erie, Albany and Hillsdale in northwestern Illinois.

The Mississippi once turned at Albany to flow to what is now Rock River.

The old river bed was known to the pioneers as "the Docia" or "the Meredosia."

Both the Rock and Mississippi rivers flooded the area until a dike was built near Albany at the upper end of the Meredosia, closing off the Mississippi River. Now the area is flooded by the Rock River. (The Rock River drains an area in Illinois of about 2,150 square miles.)

In the early days Erie, founded about 1850, would be an island for several weeks in the spring nearly every year as it was surrounded by floodwaters. As the floods abated, the lowlands became bogs and sloughs where numerous wild ducks, geese, brant (small, dark-colored geese) and cranes found places to breed.

The slough created there became a famed trapping and hunting territory where sportsmen from the East had hunting lodges. King Edward VII, former Prince of Wales, was said to have been a hunting guest in a lodge on the Docia.

A riverboat pilot, Capt. Stephen Hanks, described the Meredosia, in an account of flooding in 1881, as a "sluggish stream or mere rivulet in long dry seasons but at other times it developed into a mighty torrent. It is a natural channel between Rock River and the Mississippi and it has a valley some places five miles wide."

This swamp area or morass, home for wildfowl and animals, was a paradise hunting ground for the Indians and later the white man.

"Now," he wrote, "it is fast losing its old time character as an immense dike has been built across its mouth and another one nine miles south at what is called the 'divide.' The country is now rapidly becoming farms and meadows much of it being the richest of soil capable of growing one hundred bushels of corn per acre.

"For ages past," wrote Capt. Hanks, "the Mississippi and Rock River have rolled their floods through this great reach. Several times within the recollection of the white settlers, Rock River has gorged with ice just below where the 'Dosia' opens into it. The backed up water of the Rock would flow over the divide and come to the Mississippi in an irresistible torrent tearing out bridges and in one instance engulfing a railroad train."

Q: **How many miles wide is the Mississippi River?**

A: The width of the river varies greatly, and so do the stats!

For example, at its beginning in Lake Itasca, Minn., the river is between 20 and 30 feet wide, according to the Minnesotans. Other sources say the river there is only 10 to 12 feet.

The widest part is said by some to be just downstream from the point where the Mississippi and the Missouri meet (near Alton, Ill.) where it is nearly 1 mile (5,280 feet) across. The Mississippi River Parkway Commission claims the widest point stretches nearly four miles across near Clinton, Iowa.

We wondered how wide the river is here (when not flooding) but couldn't find a definitive statistic. (Let us know

if you have one.) Crossing the river at Interstate 74 it's 7/10 of a mile.

By the way, length measurements are even worse. For example, staff at Itasca State Park says the Mississippi is 2,552 miles long. The U.S. Geologic Survey says 2,300 miles, the EPA says 2,320 and the Mississippi National River and Recreation Area says 2,350.

Q: **There seem to be an unusual number of Turkey Vultures this year. I do not recall ever seeing any around before, and this year, I see one or groups of as many as eight almost every day. Is there a reason for this sudden increase in their population in this area?**

A: Thanks for an interesting question! We learned some fascinating facts about "TVs." Here's one from the Turkey Vulture Society:

"The Turkey Vulture's digestive system has the unique ability to kill any virus and bacteria in the food the bird eats.

A turkey vulture in flight. (Photo / file)

The vulture's droppings and dry pellets are clean and do not carry disease. This was proven by the United States Department of Agriculture in tests performed during a hog cholera epidemic in the deep South ...

"One of our more important studies concerns the proven ability of the vulture's digestive system to kill bacteria or virus in infected meat. The ability to disinfect rodent carcasses carrying Hantavirus will be tested.

"This work could be of great significance to human medical research. There may also be vital information to be discovered for use in the event of biological warfare, acts of terrorism, or world wide epidemics."

Now, back to your original question. Here's one answer, from Richard Fristik, a biologist with the U.S. Army Corps of Engineers Rock Island District:

"Many factors may affect bird populations at any given time. One interesting thing I learned is that Turkey Vultures are actually quite secretive. Instances have been reported of people not having ever seen a 'TV,' yet large, well-established roosts were located very close to their homes.

"My guess is that, similar to crows, which are becoming more common in urban areas, TVs are being forced closer to our towns and cities as large patches of woodland, where they like to roost and sometimes nest, are being lost to development. Such development may also affect the food base, although being scavengers, TVs could probably find a meal most anywhere."

Q: **Since this is the time of year for tornadoes in this area, where should a person seek shelter in their home if they have no basement? Is it safe to use a crawl space under the home?**

A: The near-universal advice for people without basements is to go to a small inner room or hallway on the lowest floor. The extra framing around bathrooms and small closets give them some additional strength, and the pipes in bathrooms offer extra anchoring.

Like most other emergency planning groups, the Federal Emergency Management Agency, on its tornado advice page, questions the wisdom of going into a crawl space. "Crawl space foundation walls are often unreinforced and therefore provide little resistance to the stresses caused by extreme winds," FEMA says.

In addition to the FEMA site listed above, The Tornado Project has an enormous amount of information about tornadoes.

Q: **I believe there is a myth or old wives' tale that when you first hear the sound of locusts, then the first frost is due in 60 days. Can you enlighten me on this?**

A: We don't know who these "old wives" are, but we've noticed they're often correct.

We believe you're really talking about *cicadas,* not locusts. (Locusts are, basically, grasshoppers.) Cicadas are those large, big-eyed insects that molt and leave their skins sticking to trees after they emerge from the ground in late summer. Then the males sit in the trees and make a LOT of noise to entertain the females.

These cicadas are called "dog-day cicadas" because they show up every year about the same time in late summer. The average date of first frost here is about Oct. 15, so when you hear the first cicadas, mark your calendar and see how they do as weather forecasters.

A good site with images and an explanation of the difference between these annual cicadas and their cousins the periodical cicadas is the Great Plains Nature Center: http://www.gpnc.org/dogday.htm.

And before anybody writes in to ask: Cicadas are *harmless*. They cannot bite or chew any plants.

Q: My wife asked me, what does "dog days" mean and how did that name come about?

A: Those are the days when your dog won't go outside because it's too hot.

No, really, the history of this term is interesting. It's named after the "dog star" Sirius, the brightest star in the sky. Sirius is in the constellation Canis Major (the Big Dog).

In late summer Sirius is in conjunction with the sun — that means it rises and sets at roughly the same time. The ancients noticed this and thought that Sirius was probably contributing to the heat of the sun and the generally hot weather. They called the period of time from 20 days before to 20 days after the conjunction "the dog days of summer" because it coincidentally fell at the time of year when it was very hot.

Today, dog days occur during the period between July 3 and August 11.

The ancients were right that Sirius is hot — it's more than 20 times brighter than our sun and twice as big. Good thing for us it's 8.7 light years away.

So, why IS it hotter right now than it was in May, or will be in October?

It's basically because the days are longer, even though Earth's aphelion (furthest point from the Sun in our orbit) was just on July 4. In other words, we're about as far away from the Sun as we get all year, but it's the hottest time of year. If you're interested in a fuller explanation, visit http://science.msfc.nasa.gov/headlines/y2002/02jul_aphelion.htm.

Q: June bugs are all over the place right now. Can they bite or sting you? What is their purpose?

A: What is their *purpose*? Even if you don't subscribe to any theological or metaphysical system, you've surely been to a Disney movie and heard the phrase "circle of life"!

Although we commonly call them June bugs, they're also called May beetles, and there are something like 100 species of the genus Phyllophaga. They are related to the dreaded Japanese beetle.

They start out as eggs laid in spring under the grass, where they promptly turn into root-eating grubs. The grubs burrow down a couple of feet for the winter, come back toward the surface in the spring to eat some more, then burrow down again, etc. They do this several times, usually three years. After a final year underground as a pupa, they come out some warm night and head for the nearest tree (or your screen door).

These beetles are entirely harmless and do not bite, so have pity. The adults are eaten by birds and the grubs fall victim to parasitic wasps and flies. For more than you wanted to know, see this site at the University of Florida: http://edis.ifas.ufl.edu/pdffiles/IN/IN20200.pdf.

ᴬ Bit of Nature

A reader adds: "June Bugs are not entirely harmless. Many years ago I was riding my new Honda 450 out in the country one hot summer night doing the then legal speed limit of 65 mph.

"I was wearing wearing a T-shirt, jeans and a helmet with a face shield but the motorcycle did not have a windshield. A June Bug hit my arm just below my shoulder. I thought I'd been shot.

"When I felt the wound with my other hand I fully expected to find blood. Luckily all I found was the remains of a large June Bug. The motorcycle had a windshield within a week! — *Bruce*

Q: At Bald Eagle Days they show immensely sized eagle nests. Here in the Q-C I see many bald eagles roost in the trees by the rivers but never see any big nests. Where do they actually build their nests?

A: Toward the end of winter, most of "our" eagles will head north for the spring and summer to nest in Minnesota, Canada and northern Wisconsin. Some stick around, though. Iowa has counted up to 60 nests, and Illinois has had about a dozen, mostly along the Mississippi River. Occasionally a pair will stay right here and nest.

Eagles like to build near water in the tallest tree in a stand. They seem to prefer conifers, also. And when they build a nest, they mean business:

The bald eagle's nest is the largest of any bird in North America — up to 6.5 feet across, three feet tall, and weighing 100 pounds.

Bald eagles mate for life and usually return to the same nest every year, expanding it a bit each season. They may nest 25 years in the same place.

One of the largest old nests recorded was nearly 10 feet across.

If you're ever lucky enough to see an eagle's nest, give the birds plenty of room and use binoculars. They will abandon a nest if humans get too close.

Q: Why are black squirrels only found in this area of the Midwest?

A: Well, we hate to burst anybody's bubble, but black squirrels aren't unique to the Quad-Cities. Council Bluffs, Iowa, and Marysville, Kan., have them.

And so do Kent State in Ohio, parts of Canada, and parks in Manhattan! Black squirrels are not a different species.

Dispatch/Argus photographer Terry Herbig caught this black squirrel feeding in his back yard.
(Photo / file)

They're a "color phase" or color variation of *Sciurus carolinensis,* the Eastern gray squirrel.

Black and gray squirrels interbreed freely, and their offspring can have a range of colors between gray and dark black.

Black squirrels are mainly found in the northern parts of the country.

Biologists think their black fur more readily absorbs the heat of the sun, a survival advantage in winter.

Students and profs who studied and counted their black squirrels on the campus at Princeton University in New Jersey figured that black coloration stayed at about 25 per cent of the grey squirrel population over the years.

Even though black squirrels are not truly rare, everyone seems to think theirs are unique.

Michigan State University officials actually have claimed that black squirrels are "native" to *their* state, and that W.W. Kellogg (think cereal) introduced them in Battle Creek.

Marysville citizens believe theirs escaped from a traveling carnival in the 1920s. Kent State students say two college staffers imported theirs from Ontario in 1961.

A Palmer family member was responsible for introducing them to the Quad-Cities, according to a book of memoirs titled "The Palmers."

"A pair of black squirrels was presented to D.D. (Palmer) by a grateful patient from Cambridge, Massachusetts," according to an excerpt from the book.

"D.D. kept them in a cage in his office building at the corner of 2nd and Brady until finally one day he mentioned the pair were being poorly treated — living in a cage — and wondered if there wasn't someplace he could let them loose."

Noted Davenport banker George Bechtel suggested calling Lt. Col. Stanhope Blunt, commander of the Rock Island Arsenal at the time, to see if Arsenal Island could serve as a new home for the squirrels.

Col. Blunt said he would be happy to have the squirrels, and after a proper ceremony, they were released on the island, according to the book.

The book suggested some of the black squirrels probably escaped the confines of Arsenal Island by crossing the Mississippi River when it was frozen.

Two last bits of trivia:

- *Sports teams at Haverford College in Pennsylvania are the Black Squirrels.*
- *The name squirrel comes the Greek skiouro or "he who sits in the shadow of his tail."*

Q: Why do they call cobwebs cobwebs? Are they not just dusty spider webs?

A: Yes, they are. Cobwebs are simply irregularly shaped webs made by Cobweb Spiders (Theridiidae). The sticky silk these spiders use does gather dust.

These spiders build inside and also outdoors in protected places. They're also called the "comb-footed" group because they have a row of bristles on their legs that they use to help wrap their prey in silk.

The black widow is a member of this family. But don't panic. There are hundreds of spiders in this group. More often, cobwebs belong to the harmless common house spider.

By the way, the word *cobweb* comes from Middle English *coppe* for spider.

Q: What effect does snow and cold have on the robins that are early in their return to our area? What do they eat besides worms? Can they find food and survive in bad weather?

A: Unless we have a heavy ice storm, they'll survive, local birdwatchers tell us. In fact, some of the robins have been here all winter anyhow.

In summer, robins eat worms, grubs, and other insects. In winter, those that remain up north switch to berries and sometimes suet from birdfeeders.

Their diet includes the fruit of hawthorn, buckthorn, mountain ash, yew, holly, wild grapes, cedar, crabapple, sumac, and multiflora rose.

You can offer overwintering robins fruit such as apple slices, raisins (soaked), blueberries, strawberries, raspberries, and cherries. Some people have tried feeding robins mealworms (available at pet stores), but it's tricky. If the mealworms freeze or get covered with snow, the robins won't notice them.

By the way, the birds who tough it out all winter have an advantage — they'll stake out the best nesting territories ahead of the ones who are returning from the South.

Q: When is the peak of morel mushroom season in the Quad-Cities? I used to hunt them with my parents as a child. I know that it requires a rainy period followed by warm weather.

A: We asked Bob Groene, outdoor writer for The Dispatch and The Rock Island Argus. He said the peak varies due to soil temperature and moisture; many people have "barometers," such as when the wild phlox or lilacs bloom or when oak leaves are the size of a squirrel's ear.

A morel mushroom.
(Photo / file)

"My experience is that the week before Mother's Day is often a very good time to head for the woods," he said.

Mr. Groene also cautioned to always make sure that you have permission to be on privately owned land, and because morel season coincides with spring wild turkey hunting season, wear a blaze-orange hat when hunting mushrooms.

A reader's comment: "As a follow-up on the morel mushroom comment on blaze-orange hat: a blaze-orange vest or other outer upper garment would even be better. Clothing colors to avoid are red, white and blue, since these are the colors of a courting tom turkey head, the preferred target of most turkey hunters. This ban on red, white and blue is not only for all exposed clothing, but also handkerchiefs. Waving around a handkerchief while blowing your nose not only attracts a tom turkey's attention but also a hunter."

Q: What's the deal with the little beetles that look like ladybugs and are everywhere these days? I have heard that the government imported them to Ohio to eat some kind of corn mite. Can this be true?

A: Yes, it's true. Those extremely annoying insects that we're all trying to get out of our homes came here with an invitation.

The Asian lady beetle Harmonia axyridis is an aphid predator in its native territory. The beetles were released several times in North America, beginning in 1916, with the idea that they would get rid of many crop pests.

The first established population wasn't seen until 1988 in Louisiana, but the beetles spread fast after that.

^ABit of Nature

As far as farmers and growers are concerned, H. axyridis is doing the job on pests of various crops, including corn borers and corn leaf aphids.

Problem is, it evidently didn't occur to anybody that H. axyridis might have a downside. We all know better now. The Asian beetles are now verging on pest status off the farm. Not only do they have the annoying habit of congregating and overwintering in homes, but some people have developed an allergic reaction to them.

(It may have been inevitable: Some scientists believe that the current populations of H. axyridis did not come from the deliberate releases, but from Asian beetles riding ships into U.S. seaports.)

Why have they gotten worse in the Midwest so quickly, you might wonder? (We did.) Well, in 2000, there were large outbreaks of soybean aphid. The beetle population followed this food source and multiplied dramatically.

No great relief is in sight, that we can find. Scientists have bred a strain of wingless Asian lady beetles, although not necessarily with the idea of keeping them out of your house. The plan is to force them to hang around the field and eat more aphids.

Q: In response to the lady beetle question, I noted the response said they do not sting. I noted the other day that they do bite. Is this true, or am I imagining it?

A: Maybe they do, maybe they don't … According to the U of Illinois, "Although they may bite, they do not injure humans, nor can they breed or

reproduce indoors." The U of Indiana says "ladybugs characteristically do not bite, sting or carry diseases." The U of Ohio says "These beetles do not bite or sting …"

Q: Why are we seeing so many ladybugs, and is there anything we can do to get rid of them? They discolor the siding on your house, and on your walls inside the house.

A: The Iowa State University Entomolgy Department feels your pain. Here's what their experts say:

"Several of the common species of lady beetles (ladybugs, if you prefer) found in Iowa will wander indoors during the fall. However, this is a dis-

Asian ladies feed on a leaf.
(Photo / file)

tinctive and annoying trait of the Asian lady beetle, a relatively new species imported to the United States from eastern Asia. The multicolored Asian lady beetle *(pictured)* (Harmonia axyridis), has become common in many areas of the eastern U.S. and most of Iowa. This biological control natural enemy is a beneficial inhabitant of the landscape but can also be a serious household pest in those areas where it has become well established and abundant.

"Asian lady beetles, like box-elder bugs, are accidental invaders; that is, 'outdoor' insects that create a nuisance by wandering indoors during a limited portion of their life cycle. Accidental invaders do not feed or reproduce indoors. They cannot attack the house structure, furniture, or fabric. They cannot sting or carry diseases. Lady beetles may leave a slimy smear, and they have a distinct odor when squashed.

"The most effective management option is to prevent invasion by sealing cracks, gaps and openings on the outside during late summer. Application of synthetic pyrethroid insecticides such as permethrin to the outside of buildings may help prevent pest entry. Treatment must be applied before the beetles begin to enter buildings to be effective (mid to late October in east-central Iowa). Homeowner insecticides other than permethrin usually do not provide satisfactory prevention.

"The practical solution for homeowners in fall and winter is to vacuum and discard invader lady beetles as they appear."

Ohio State entomologists agree. "Remove beetles from inside the home with a broom and dust pan and/or vacuum cleaner. Collect the beetles from indoors and deposit them outside, perhaps under a bush or in some other covered area well away from any homes. Please do not kill them. Beetles saved may return the favor by eating harmful aphids from your vegetable and ornamental plants later in the season." (Note: The Convergent Lady Beetle became the official Ohio state insect in 1975.)

University of Illinois experts say the Asian ladybugs are more apt to come inside now than other types because, in their homeland of China, they inhabit tall cliffs to overwinter. "As you know, there are very few tall cliffs in Illinois, so the next best thing is a building."

Don't squash them. If crushed, the beetles will emit a foul odor and leave a stain.

Q: I'm 62 years old and recently I have noticed a number of "age spots" (brownish spots similar to freckles) on my face. In addition to the sun, can sunless tanning lotion bring these out also?

A: No. Age spots, or liver spots as some call them, are caused primarily by exposure to the sun. The chemicals used in sunless tanning will not create more age spots, and usually won't affect the ones you have now.

We found an interesting message board at sunless.com and asked your question. Here's what one of their moderators, Vicki, says:

"In most cases it (sunless tanning) will not affect them at all, and since surrounding skin is darkened, it can make them blend in better.

"However, if they have a rough or raised surface, then they can absorb some sunless tanner and darken temporarily, until the tan fades. But you can just dab any freshly applyed solution off of them with a Q-tip dipped in alcohol or facial taner or astringent, and that will remove any excess solution.

"You can also dab facial hair bleach on them, after tanning, to lighten any solution related darkening.

"Age spots are related to UV exposure, so the best prevention is consistant use of a good broad-coverage sunscreen EVERY DAY, rain or shine.

"Look for one that contains zinc oxide, titanium dioxide, or avobenzone (Parsol) in the active-ingredient list, with an SPF of at least 15, though 30 is better.

"This will help prevent formation of new spots, and also allow older spots to begin to fade. Though depending on the degree of damage, they may not fade much.

"I have some that have faded away through the years, but some others wont budge, even though I am scrupulouse with sunscreen usage, and limiting UV exposure."

Another contributor, Kim, said: "I actually have 3 that do get darker with ST — but then, my natural color is very, very fair — and I am also unable to add more ST to blotchy areas to even out the color, because the dark spots just get darker. So I'm guessing that it might have something to do with your skintone & the way your body reacts to ST."

We want to remind you that if any spot on your skin shows signs of change, or looks suspicious, you should have it checked by a doctor.

Q: Once or twice a year there is a full moon two times in one month. Why is this, and why different months each year?

A: A complete phase cycle of the moon (a "lunation") is 29.5 days. Because lunation is shorter than most calendar months, the phase of the moon at the beginning of the month usually repeats at the end of the month.

When there are two full moons in a month — as there is in July 2004 — the second one is called a "Blue Moon."

Our Blue Moon will be July 31. Take note, you have to wait an average of 2.7 years for another one. According to the Old Farmers Almanac, the next one will be May 2007.

Q: Where is the highest point in Mercer and Rock Island counties?

A: The highest point in Rock Island County is an unnamed hilltop near the village of Reynolds on the Rock Island/Mercer county line, according to the Illinois State Geological Survey. The hilltop is 810 feet above mean sea level.

The highest point in Mercer County is an unnamed hilltop, immediately south of Rock Island County's highest point, that's 820 feet above mean sea level, according to ISGS.

Both high points are within the same 30-meter-by-30-meter quadrangle, according is ISGS.

Q: Recently, there were news accounts about a bear sighting in eastern Iowa. When was the last reported sighting of a bear in Illinois? Is it likely there are any bears remaining in the state?

A: It's unlikely there are any black bears in Illinois, though there have been sightings this year in Iowa and Missouri.

A resident near Anaconda, Mo., spotted a black bear May 15, and wildlife experts found tracks confirming the sighting. About a week earlier, there was an unconfirmed report of a bear near Washington, Mo. Wildlife experts believe it was the same bear. The locations are roughly 50 miles southwest of St. Louis.

A Bit of Nature

In May and June, there were confirmed sightings of black bears near Solon and Marengo in Iowa, in the area between Iowa City and Cedar Rapids.

Sightings also were reported in Benton, Clayton and Buchanan counties in Iowa. Other bears, which presumably wander down from Minnesota, have occasionally been seen in northeast Iowa over the past decade.

Black bears were seen frequently in the 1700s in Illinois but were rare by the mid-1850s. The last few bears were seen in 1855 in Massac County in Southern Illinois. Black bears were extinct in Illinois by 1866, and there are no plans of reintroducing them into the state.

(Thanks to Trevor Lawrence of the Illinois Division of Wildlife Program Development for his assistance on this question.)

Bits and Pieces of History

Q: I've been told there's a Confederate cemetery at the site of what was the Rock Island Civil War Prison. As a Civil War buff, I'm curious about how many Confederate soldiers are buried there and if the cemetery is open to visitors.

A: There are 1,960 Confederate soldiers in the Confederate Cemetery, a separate enclave of the National Cemetery on Arsenal Island. The first Confederate prisoners arrived on the island Dec. 23, 1863. Approximately 12,000 eventually passed through the prison camp before the Civil War ended, with the maximum number at any time being 8,594.

The first burials in what became Rock Island National Cemetery were Union soldiers who served as guards at the camp.

The cemetery is open to visitors. For more information, see the Visiting Rock Island Arsenal page on the Arsenal Web site.

Q: When did Lindbergh bring the Spirit of St. Louis to Moline after his solo transatlantic flight in 1927?

A: Charles Lindbergh landed the Spirit of St. Louis in Moline on Aug. 19, 1927, some three months after his fabled solo journey across the Atlantic.

Contemporary newspaper accounts estimated that 150,000 people greeted the "Lone Eagle" at the airport or along the route of a parade through the Quad-Cities.

The number seems fantastic, given that the total population of Scott and Rock Island counties at the time was about 170,000. But it's difficult to overstate the awe with which the world viewed Lindbergh and his flying feat, and people likely came from many miles to see him.

That night, some 1,200 people jammed into the Rock Island Arsenal Golf Club for a dinner at which Lindbergh was guest of honor. Dr. G. A. Andreen, president of Augustana College, was principal speaker. Lindbergh, "obviously a little shy, a little tired and a little overcome by the glowing greeting," spoke only briefly, The Dispatch reported. He thanked his hosts, praised the local airport and

Charles Lindbergh and the Spirit of St. Louis at the Moline Airport Aug. 20, 1927, just before take-off. (Photo/file)

Charles Lindbergh, center, in a leather jacket, posed with Quad-Cities dignitaries Aug. 19, 1927. From the left are Col. D.M. King, commandant of the Rock Island Arsenal; East Moline Mayor John H. Siefken; Moline Mayor C. W. Sandstrom; Lindbergh; Davenport Mayor L. A. Roddewig and Rock Island Mayor Chester C. Thompson. (Photo / file)

urged the community to continue its progress on the aviation front.

Lindberg spent the night with Col. D.M. King, commandant at Rock Island Arsenal, and departed the next day, Aug. 20.

Moline was one of 92 cities into which Lindberg flew the Spirit of St. Louis from July 20 to Oct. 23, 1927. The tour, sponsored by the Daniel Guggenheim Fund for the Promotion of Aeronautics, covered 48 states and 22,000 air miles and saw Lindbergh give 147 speeches and ride in 1,290 miles of parades.

An interesting sidelight to the visit was an apparent hoax story and photo in the Davenport Times, the story purporting to be an interview with Lindbergh and the photo purporting to be one of the Spirit of St. Louis flying over the Mississippi between Rock Island and Davenport. The problem was that the paper containing the story and photo

appeared on the streets before Lindbergh's arrival, and the aviator denounced it when it was called to his attention. "Lindbergh says Davenport paper published fake" read a headline in The Dispatch the next day.

Before departing Aug. 20, Lindbergh posed for a farewell photo by Dispatch photographer Charles Ekstrom, "provided it not be given or loaned to the Davenport newspaper that caused him the annoyance the day before."

Q: "The Dolly" train wrecked near New Boston on March 27, 1909. What caused the wreck? I was told it was cattle, I tried to verify it but cannot find any information. Could you please help?

A: A May 7, 1995, feature story in The Argus/Dispatch about "The Dolly" said the wreck was caused when the tender car jumped the track, pulling the engine with it. The engineer, Thomas Jenks of Galesburg, was severely scalded and died a few hours later. Two other people were injured.

"The Dolly" carried passengers and freight in Mercer, Henry, Henderson and Knox counties for 82 years, before it was discontinued in 1952, the story said.

There's a photo of the wreck on Augustana College's Web site: http://sparc5.augustana.edu/library/train7.gif.

Q: I was browsing through your archives and saw the section about Mr. Looney. I know you're not supposed to believe

everything you see in the movies but the movie "Road to Perdition" greatly differs from your version. What gives? Also … is the house/hotel that John Looney lived in still around? I heard a rumor that it was and that it is open for tours.

A: What gives is that the movie-makers based the film *very* loosely on the real-life John Looney. The film was actually an adaptation of "Road to Perdition," a graphic novel by Max Collins of Muscatine, who made no pretense that his work was historically accurate. The stories in the Looney package from The Argus/Dispatch comprise the most accurate account of the gangster's career that we're aware of. You can read them at http://www.qconline.com/more/loon ey/looneyhed.html.

The Looney house is still around. We're not aware that it's open for tours.

Q: Does anyone know when the John Deere Foundry on 9th Street in Silvis was built? And why it shut down?

A: The foundry was built in 1966-68, at a cost of $30 million. The state-of-the-art plant was ranked as one of the 10 best foundries in the country at the time.

It produced iron for Deere products and for those of other manufacturers, including Ford and Caterpillar.

After a revamp that sharply increased capacity, the foundry hit its all-time high of 1,450 employees in 1981. But a major downtown in farm equipment sales dropped both in-house and outsides sales and sent employment on a downard spiral. By

1991, the foundry was running at less than 50 percent capacity and was losing money, Deere officials said in announcing that the company would phase out operations there.

Deere consolidated foundry operations at its Waterloo foundry. The Silvis operation shut down for good March 31, 1993, eliminating the remaining 575 jobs.

Q: When I was a kid living in Rock Island in the 1930s, there was a steam-driven, sternwheel ferryboat. It ran between Rock Island and Davenport. What was the name of the boat? What was its history, and what happend to it?

A: The ferry you recall was probably the W. J. Quinlan.

Marlene Gantt, author of the "Images of the Past" column in The Dispatch, has written that the Quinlan was built in 1904 by Fred Kahlke in Rock Island.

It was originally named the Davenport but got a new name when W. J. Quinlan purchased it in 1925. In addition to serving as a ferry, it had a storied career as a cruise boat featuring music, dancing and dining.

The Quinlan was destroyed by fire while in drydock at the Kahlke Boatyard in Rock Island in 1967.

A reader adds: "Re: the W.J. Quinlan — My father rode on it and played with the band while his Mom and Dad shopped in Davenport. He said it was a great 'baby sitter.' (It cost a nickel then.) I have been trying to locate additional information on Mr. Ralph Law, who the Times-Democrat labeled as America's foremost painter of steamboats. I have a signed print by Mr. Law (39/100) of the Quinlan that was distributed through WOC-TV (circa 1970s) and also wonder about the history of that print. Personally, I also fished in and around the inlet where the Quinlan was drydocked prior to the fire; as well as off the Quinlan itself. I was chased off numerous times by 'old man Kahlke.' Thanks for the reminiscence!" — *Kenneth L. Knapp, Fox Lake, Ill. (A native Quad-Citian)*

W. J. Quinlan

Q: **Does anyone know where I might find pictures of the W. J. Quinlan? I also played on the boat back in the '50s. I also have a painting of her by an artist in Rock Island. I was born in 1940 and lived there until 1955.**

A: We found a couple of pictures of the W. J. Quinlan, both from the library of The Dispatch. Neither is dated.

The Quinlan is probably the best known of the many ferries that operated between Rock Island and Davenport before the Centennial Bridge opened to traffic in 1940. Built

W. J. Quinlan

in Rock Island in 1904, it was named The Davenport until 1925, when Willian J. Quinlan purchased it. Used as a cruise boat as well as a ferry, the Quinlan was famed for its entertainment — music, dancing, a bar, bingo and, it is said, slot machines.

The Quinlan stayed in business until 1946, when, losing money and judged unseaworthy, it was docked at the Kahlke Boatyard in Rock Island. It burned there in 1967, depriving Rock Island kids of what was apparently a favorite spot.

We've heard several tales from people who described how, as teens or pre-teens, they managed to sneak onto the drydocked Quinlan for some play time.

Q: **What year did the Quad City Downs break ground and start building?**

A: Our best estimate is 1970, though we've been unable to pin down the exact date.

The files in our library for that era are incomplete, but we found references to the track in 1969 that indicated construction had not yet begun.

The track opened May 2, 1973, after the Illinois Racing Board at a meeting in the fall of 1972 awarded racing dates. It's unlikely the racing dates would have been awarded unless the track was ready.

We quizzed a couple of old-timers who were active in East Moline city government at the time, and they, too, were unsure of the exact year but suggested that 1969 or 1970 was right. Perhaps one of our readers can provide a more precise answer.

The track, incidentally, was known as East Moline Downs when it opened.

A reader adds: "I grew up in East Moline and have a distinct memory of the ... beginnings of QC Downs. The race track had to be voted on because the city would have to provide electricity, water and sewerage and pave a road to the track. There may also have been a bond issue on the ballot. The voters defeated the proposed measure twice. They did not want to pay for a race track, and some folks opposed it due to their beliefs about the wrongness of gambling. Well, the city council approved it anyway ... This occurred during my senior year at UTHS in 1972-1973.

"... one of only two happy endings to it all was that the race track lost money in its first year and went bankrupt. The track was sold. The original directors of the track all lost money and were booted out by the new owners. I believe that is why the track changed names. The only other happy circumstance to all this was that the resignation of the former mayor allowed Denny Jacobs to run, be elected and serve as the wonderful mayor he was for East Moline for so many years. Thanks for the great job you do."

Q: What exactly is the "Grand Excursion"? How was it originally started? It may have been described in the past, but there are some people who do not remember or were not around then. Thank You.

A: The "Grand Excursion" that's in the news these days is a 150th anniversary re-creation of an 1854 event celebrating the completion of a railroad to Rock Island.

Some 1,200 dignitaries, including former President Millard Fillmore, rode the Rock Island Lines to Rock Island, then boarded steamboats for a river journey to Minneapolis-St. Paul. The event, of course, also was intended to spur migration by spotlighting the lands that were being made more readily accessible.

Plans for the 2004 Grand Excusion have been under way since 2000.

Dozens of communities along the river are involved.

Q: I have heard that there was a German prisoner-of-war camp near Fairport, Iowa, just south of the Quad-Cities, where the state fish hatcheries are now. Any truth to that?

A: Yes, it's true. There was a German POW camp at the Fairport Fish Hatchery, near Muscatine. It was one of 34 camps administered from a "hub" camp in Algona, a small town in north central Iowa. More than 10,000 German prisoners passed through the hub camp, which housed about 3,000 prisoners and dispatched the remainder to smaller camps in a four-state area.

According to the Algona P.W. Camp Web site (http://powcamp.algona. org/), "the Muscatine, Ia., branch was housed in a solid three-story brick fish hatchery near Fairport."

The Web site named above is maintained by the Algona Chamber of Commerce, which is assembling as much information as possible about the "empire," which "reached 285 miles east of Algona to Clinton; 220 miles south to Shenandoah; 185 miles west to Onawa and almost 500 miles north to Grafton, North Dakota."

The site also says that "The kind of work that the PWs performed was as varied as the communities they lived in. They served farmers, worked in canneries, nurseries, milk processing plants and a box and barrel factory. They detasseled hybrid corn for DeKalb and Pioneer in Humboldt and Algona. They cut timber and pulpwood in northern Minnesota. They worked in brick and tile factories, did silo construction, cleared drainage ditches of scrub trees and, in two camps, were employed in the unpleasant work of eviscerating chickens."

The site also has camp-related photos, letters, newspaper articles and more.

Q: Al Jolson was the greatest entertainer of the 20th century. Did he ever perform in the Quad-Cities?

A: As it turns out, the famous singer visited the Quad-Cities many times. Mr. Jolson, of course, was the star of a pioneering "talkie," the 1927 film "The Jazz Singer." He was also one of the best-known and loved performers of his time.

Al Jolson (Photo / file)

We're indebted to Mark Leavy, webmaster for the The International Al Jolson Society and A.J.Recordings (http://www.jolson.org/) for his help. If you interested in Mr. Jolson, be sure to visit this very informative site.

Here are dates we know about: On Feb. 12-17, 1906, Mr. Jolson played at the People's Theater in Cedar Rapids; then Feb. 19-24 that year he was at the Garrick in Burlington, so he may have passed through Davenport.

During a vaudeville tour on the Sullivan & Considine Circuit, he played April 15-20, 1907, at the Elite in Davenport.

With Lew Dockstader's Minstrels, he played Oct. 11, 1908, at the Burtis Opera House in Davenport, then on to Burlington, Cedar Rapids, and Sioux City. He returned with the Minstrels on Oct. 20, 1909, to the Burtis in Davenport again. He then went to Galesburg, Ill, and may have gone through Rock Island.

Mr. Jolson brought his Broadway show "Dancing Around" to the Burtis in Davenport on Sept. 27, 1915. By then he was a major star. He brought his next show, "Robinson Crusoe Jr.," to the Burtis on Sept. 27, 1917.

"The Wonder Bar," Mr. Jolson's last show that toured in the 1930s, was at the Masonic Temple in Davenport on Feb. 21, 1932.

Al Jolson also was a guest at the Harper House in Rock Island on at least one occasion, but we don't know the date. The hotel was at the corner of 2nd Avenue and 19th Street from 1881 to 1973. (Its guest list also included Buffalo Bill Cody and the 1919 Chicago White Sox.)

Q: I went to high school at the old Winola High School in Viola, Ill., and it closed the summer before my senior year. I moved away from the QC right after graduation. What has happened to the school since it closed in

1988? Is anyone actively using the building?

A: We checked with Viola Village Board President Kirk Doonan, who said that, yes, the old high school building is still standing and that parts of it are still in use.

He said the building has had two or three sets of owners since the school was shut down in 1988. The gymnasium housed a plastics factory for a while, but it's gone now.

At the moment, there's a family gymnasium in what was the school's cafeteria. The remainder of the building is mostly used for storage, Mr. Doonan said.

Q: A CD called "Civil War and Iowa" lists military camps in Davenport. Besides Camp McClellan, which everyone knows about, four others are listed — Roberts (later named Kinsman), Joe Holt, Herron and Hendershott. My question is, do you know where these camps were located in the City of Davenport?

A: The American Forts of the West Web site (http://www.geocities.com/naforts) lists seven Davenport camps, including those you named and two others. Here they are:

- *Camp Herron (1862), located between present-day Farnam Street and Churchill's Addition.*
- *Camp McClellan (1861 - 1865), located on the riverfront at Lindsay Park.*
- *Camp Kearny (1863 - 1865), a prison stockade adjacent to Camp McClellan for Sioux Indians captured after the Sioux Uprising in Minnesota.*
- *Camp Roberts (1863), located on Duck Creek, later renamed Camp Kinsman,*

marked on Eastern Avenue.
- *Camp Hendershott (1862), between 13th, Locust, Ripley, and Scott streets.*
- *Camp Joe Holt (1861), located at the old fairgrounds between 13th, Perry, and Rock Island streets and Northern Avenue. (Kirkwood Boulevard).*
- *Camp Black Hawk, a cavalry camp. Undetermined location.*

Q: Is there a book on the murder James Klindt committed?

A: Yes. Two Davenport men, Pat Gipple and Matthew Clemens, published "Dead Water — The Klindt Affair" in 1995.

As you probably know, James Klindt was convicted of killing his wife, Joyce, and dumping her torso in the Mississippi River. He was released from prison March 13, 2004 — five days shy of the 21st anniversary of her death.

At the time of the crime, the Klindts had lived for seven years in what was known as the "castle house" on Royal Oaks Drive in Davenport. They were divorcing when Joyce Klindt disappeared.

The night before she disappeared, she made an audiotape of an argument with her husband. He could be heard on the tape threatening to cut her into "little pieces."

One month later, fishermen found a torso in the Mississippi River. The body had been cut at the thighs and navel with a chain saw. James Klindt was arrested a little more than a year later, taken from his chiropractic clinic on the first floor of his parents' home in Davenport.

Here's an excerpt from a 1995 review of the book by Murray Hancks, editorial page editor at The Rock Island Argus:

"The Klindt murder case was spectacular for several reasons. First, of course, was the way Mrs. Klindt was killed.

"As we are now seeing in the O.J. Simpson murder trial in California, genetic testing played a critical role in Dr. Klindt's trial. Because there were no witnesses to the murder, prosecutors had to rely on a small tissue sample from the torso to determine that the victim was Mrs. Klindt. The introduction of genetic testing in the case set precedent and actually made law.

"But there were other reasons why the case proved so dramatic.

"There was the steamy love affair between Dr. Klindt and Davenport woman Terry Keuhn; there was the dogged police investigation by Davenport police detective Lt. Ted Carroll; there was the courtroom drama of Scott County Attorney William E. Davis; and there was the diligent and descriptive media coverage of Mrs. Klindt's disappearance, the discovery of the torso, Dr. Klindt's two trials (the first one in Keokuk ended in a hung jury), and his conviction and sentencing.

"Authors Gipple and Clemons spent two-and-a-half years to research the 269-page Klindt book.

" 'Because this was our first attempt at non-fiction, the hardest part was staying out of people's heads,' said Mr. Gipple, a stockbroker with Beyer & Co., Davenport. 'I would guess we have 9,000 to 10,000 hours in this book. Even if we had a best seller, we'd make minimum wage.'

"Mr. Clemens, a professional writer who runs Pro Text Ltd., Davenport, said writing the book was a wonderful experience. 'So much was written and said about the murder, we knew we had to do a book,' he said. 'We owe a lot to Davenport police officer Rick Chase and Bill Davis for their help.

Bill provided us with an 80-pound box of material about the case and gave us five or six hours of interviews. And Rick's memory was amazing.'

"The authors also relied on newspaper clippings from the case. They said former Rock Island Argus reporter Judy Pochel's coverage of the case was invaluable.

"James Klindt — who has since confessed to the crime — was not interviewed for the book. However, the authors said they have spoken recently with the convicted killer, who told them he is interested in reading the book. 'He said he was happy that most of the book came from court transcripts,' Mr. Gipple said.

" 'Dead Water' is an accurate account of the Klindt case. From the disappearance of Joyce Klindt to James Klindt's conviction, the book covers the case step by step. Readers will find that once they pick the book up, they won't want to put it down."

Q: I recently did the cemetery walk at Riverside and at least three different times during the re-enactment, they mentioned the Turner Association. What was this association? When did it form? Who originated it? The reason for my interest is, my mother's maiden name was Turner.

A: The re-enactors were referring to the American Turners, an organization brought to this country by Germans who came here in the late 1840s and after. A teacher, Friedrich Ludwig Jahn (1778-1852), founded the Turner movement in Germany. The Turners have a long and fascinating history. Their societies combined gymnastics with politics and personal freedom ("A Sound Mind in a Sound Body"), which eventually got them in trouble in their homeland and led many of them to come here.

When the Turners established societies in the U.S., they eventually added more to their organizations, including music and social activities, and began including women.

They were once very active in the Quad-Cities area but have faded away. Ruth Reynolds, administrative assistant at the German American Heritage Center in Davenport, said the last Iowa-side Turners Club disbanded recently. She said that, as far as she knows, none of the clubs remain on the Illinois side either.

Turnen is a word coined by Jahn, meaning "to perform gymnastic exercises." How, or if it's related to your mother's name, we don't know.

The German American Heritage Center, 712 W. 2nd St.,offers an exhibit, "150Years of Turners." It's open Saturday and Sunday from 1 to 4 p.m.

An architect's sketch of the Builders Lumber Co. building, which later housed Sportsland Family Fun Center Marine Supplies, Sales and Service. (Photo / file)

was sold to Hardees and demolished to make room for the restaurant that's on the corner now.

Q: There was a boat store on 23rd Avenue and 41st Street in Moline when I was a small child, where Hardees is now. What happened to it?

A: The Sportsland Family Fun Center Marine Supplies, Sales and Service was sold in 1979 to Beacon Bay Boats, which, so far as we can determine, is no longer in business.

The round, glass-walled building, one of the most distinctive in the Quad-Cities, was constructed for Builders' Lumber Co. in the 1950s.

After Sportsland sold out, the building was occupied by Supreme TV and Appliances until 1989, when it

Q: I live on Vandruff's Island in Milan. Can you tell me a little bit about the history of the island and about Joshua Vandruff?

A: A little bit — Joshua Vandruff was among the area's earliest settlers, kept cattle, trafficked in whiskey and had a large family.

He arrived here in 1828, the first year white settlers moved into what is now Rock Island County. He must have been an irritant to the Native Americans from the beginning.

John Henry Hauberg, an early 20th-century historian, relates that Black Hawk, "perceiving the damaging effect of whiskey on his people," went to the Vandruff home and "knocked in the heads" of Vandruff's whiskey barrels.

David Sears, a descendant of early settler David B. Sears, also mentioned the incident in a 1917 memoir. He referred to "the house where Black Hawk spilled the whiskey." He said Ben Goble, a Vandruff son-in-law, told him about the incident.

Sears also wrote that "The Vandruffs were frontier people, very sociable, always ready to accept favors, not very ambitious."

Judge John Spencer, another early resident, described another incident, this one from 1831, the year before the Black Hawk War: "Black Hawk said we could all stay this season, except Joshua Vandruff and Rinnah Wells, who lived in the midst of their village and had a large stock of cattle, which troubled the Indians a great deal. Mr. Vandruff showed Black Hawk that it would be very hard for him to leave on so short a notice, as he was a poor man and had twelve children."

Black Hawk finally consented that he could stay another season, but Mr. Wells must go.

David B. Sears, whose dams on Sylvan Slough helped attract John Deere to the area, moved to Vandruff's Island in 1867 and built power dams and a variety of factories there.

Q: **I have questions about two crimes that occurred when I was a young boy in Rock Island. Both incidents involved friends of mine. The first was the murder of Jeff Ramsey. The second was the abduction of a grade-school-aged friend and neighbor, Heather Bailey. I have only fully realized the effects the impact of these crimes had on my life now that I'm an adult and a parent. I am not certain of the accuracy of my memories.**

A: The murder of Jeff Ramsey was never solved. The kidnapper of Heather Bailey was caught, convicted and is still serving time for another crime.

The details:

Ralph LaVerne Doughty

Heather Bailey was 7 years old in 1975 when she was kidnapped by a man named Ralph LaVerne Doughty in Rock Island.

The girl and some friends were lured out of their neighborhood by Doughty on June 8. He told them he needed their help searching for his daughter in a wooded area near Hauberg Civic Center. Doughty and the girl subsequently disappeared and the other children sounded the alarm. Heather was found, unharmed, about five hours later at the man's apartment.

Doughty was sentenced to 8-20 years in prison after pleading guilty to aggravated kidnapping. At the time, prosecutors said records showed Doughty also had been convicted on at least two "morals" charges in Iowa.

He served about four years.

In August 1983, Doughty was sentenced to life in prison for the first-degree kidnapping of a 5-year-old boy in Davenport who was on his way to school.

The boy, who was sexually assaulted, told police he was lured away from school by a man claiming to be looking for a lost dog.

However, in December 1984, the Iowa Supreme Court overturned the conviction because of the way the jury instructions were given.

A second trial, and second conviction ensued. In February 1987, Doughty, then 41, again was sentenced to life without parole. He is incarcerated at Anamosa State Penitentiary.

The nude body of 12-year-old Jeff Ramsey was found under a pile of debris on the south side of Arsenal Island on June 15, 1972, about 25 feet from the edge of Sylvan Slough.

The Rock Island boy had been reported missing a week earlier. He had been on his way to the river to watch the fishermen.

A nylon cord was wrapped around his neck, and the autopsy showed he died from strangulation. He also had been beaten. Officials believed he had been sexually abused, but his body was too badly decomposed for tests to show that.

Jeff Ramsey

Although rewards were offered, no informants ever came forward. The boy's parents did receive three or four anonymous letters in the following days from someone claiming to be the killer.

One letter said: "I did it, my God I did it, I killed him." The writer said he needed help, and the family responded with an open letter in the newspapers to the writer, asking him to call police.

Some time later the writer sent his last message, saying that he'd already gotten help, but "If I ever have the urge again, I'll kill myself before I do this again."

Speculation ran high for a time that Jeff's death was connected with a carnival that had been playing on the Davenport levee at the time. Other young boys in Illinois, Iowa and Indiana also had disappeared about the same time carnivals were in their towns. FBI agents spent a year tracing carnival workers without finding a lead.

In the spring of 1976, the FBI closed the case. The only suspect in the case, who was a Quad-Cities resident but never identified, had killed himself.

Senior FBI agent Charles Smith said in an interview in 1978 that agents interviewed the prime suspect twice but didn't have enough evidence to make an arrest. "This was probably the most frustrating case I've ever worked on," he said.

Q: **Tell me about Allendale, the place where the Moline Board of Education has its offices. What is the history of the house, etc.?**

A: In short, the mansion was built for Mr. And Mrs. Frank G. Allen in 1906. The Allens donated it to the school district in 1931.

Here's a story about Allendale from the Dispatch/Argus Progress '98 edition:

Allendale, an office with charm
MOLINE — Allendale normally bustles with the activities of the Moline schools administration office.

However, during winter break with staff on vacation and most offices quiet, it is a perfect time to poke around the 91-year-old mansion from top to bottom.

The English Tudor house at 1619 11th Ave., stands on a bluff overlooking Moline's downtown. The interior layout has remained relatively similar to the house the school district took over. Only a few interior walls and doorways have been added, as well as a wing on the west side of the house.

Allendale, donated to the Moline schools by Frank and Minnie Allen in 1931, is one of several majestic turn-of-the-century houses that dot the hills overlooking the Quad-Cities. It received an award from the Moline Preservation Society in 1997.

The Allens also built houses for their children across from Allendale on 11th Avenue. A garage and other outbuildings on the west side of the estate now are privately owned.

The house features amazing views, interesting nooks and fascinating crannies, all pointed out by tour guide and Moline superintendent Ben McAdams. A tour is a rare treat. Short tours usually only are given to Scout troops and student groups.

Mr. McAdams is no stranger to the house on the hill. He served as the district's director of special services until he retired in 1988. He notes points of interest and offers as much knowledge as he can about the house.

He bounded through the snow to point out where a beloved dog, Rover, is buried on the northeast corner of the yard. The spot is marked with an engraved tombstone.

Sitting behind the desk in his office, which has one of Allendale's numerous fireplaces, Mr. McAdams said people see the house and their imagination runs wild.

"The statements I hear most is 'What was it like when the Allens lived here, what was it like at Christmastime, how many people did it take to keep clean?' " he said. "People are amazed at the intricacy of the woodworking."

The house's north face originally was the front when Frank and Minnie Allen built the house in 1906. Much of the yard now is blacktop for parking purposes. Stone steps curving down to 16th Street now are closed off.

Inside, the district has done restoration work where needed. The many fireplaces draw out the dark beauty of the woodwork. The woodwork on the first floor is the most ornate and distinctive.

In Allendale's library, now a conference room, floor-to-ceiling bookcases surround the house's most decorative fireplace. It features a coat of arms and Latin inscription "Fortiter gerit crucem," meaning "Bravely he carries the cross."

The second floor was mostly bedrooms, including the Allen's suite over the porte chochere which extends over what is now the main entrance to the house. It has windows facing south, east and west.

The house's sunroom, which is part of the west wing later added to the house, also is on the second floor. There were 22 large rooms in the house, with nine bathrooms.

The ballroom, with its arched ceiling, dominates the third floor. A billard room was off the ballroom, with a card room next to it. The music room also was connected to the ballroom.

The butler's quarters are reached through a door in the music room. Although the space mostly is used for storage, the three peaked windows of the butler's quarters provide Allendale's most spectacular view.

In the basement, there is little to see except the sizable wine cellar that now stands empty. It has a lock, which showed the owners might not have trusted the nine servants on staff. There also is a safe, reportedly placed there when the house was built because it could not fit through any doors.

Allendale has served many uses since it was donated to the school district.

It has been used for a school library annex, junior high classes, and home-economics classes. The last classes were taught at Allendale in 1958 before it became the district's administrative center. Mr. McAdams also recalls there were two apartments in the house rented to teachers.

He said he doesn't know the complete history of the house and its former occupants, acknowledging there are only bits and pieces. He said that is part of the house's charm.

"It makes you wonder what all went on in here." — *By Kurt Allemeier (January 22, 1998)*

Q: **What has become of the Plantation Restaurant, which was housed in the old Velie mansion known as Villa Velie? Has the house been preserved? It has been several years since I was in Moline, and remember fondly dining there.**

A: The Plantation is long gone, but the Velie mansion on Moline's 7th Street north of Black Hawk Road lives on — it's now the home of Quad City Bank and Trust.

The Plantation closed not long after owner Nick Chirekos was murdered in 1979.

The mansion housed other restaurants off and on through 1993. It was vacant until it was remodeled as a home for the bank, which began operations there in 1998.

Q: **Who is Casimir Pulaski, and why do my children get Casimir Pulaski Day off from school?**

A: Pulaski was born on March 4, 1747, near Warsaw, Poland, to a family of minor Polish nobility. His father was a leader of Polish rebels fighting against Russia, and Casimir fought with him. Their cause was defeated, and Casimir fled under a death sentence.

In the summer of 1776, he asked the Americans to join their forces, and at that time the Revolutionary Army was in sore need of experienced officers. Leading a charge, Pulaski sustained a fatal wound while fighting for American independence at the battle of Savannah in 1779.

Casimir Pulaski
(Photo / file)

According to John J. Kulczycki, professor of History, University of Illinois at Chicago, Pulaski has always been a hero to Americans.

"Shortly after his death, a solemn memorial service was held in Charleston, and, before the end of 1779, the Continental Congress resolved that a monument should be erected in his honor, though a statue was not put into place in Washington, D.C., until 1910," Mr. Kulczycki writes in *Casimir Pulaski 1747-1779: A Short Biography.*

"Over the years Americans have kept alive his memory, naming many counties, towns, streets, parks, and squares after him ... In his first letter to Washington, after arriving in America, Pulaski wrote, 'I came here, where freedom is being defended, to serve it, and to live or die for it.' He proved true to his word. For this, we honor him as a soldier of Liberty for all."

The Illinois Legislature voted in 1977 to make the first Monday in March of each year a holiday to be observed throughout the state and to be known as the birthday of Casimir Pulaski.

In Chicago, Gen. Pulaski is honored by a yearly parade, and named after him are Pulaski Road, Pulaski Park in the West Town community, and the Pulaski School.

We recommend that you explore the many resources about Pulaski to be found on the Web. His is a fascinating, colorful story! Some links: http://www.pulaskiparade.com/ english.html, http://www.iyp.org/ polish/history/pulaski.html, http://www.ncsa.uiuc.edu/Edu/ illinois/polish/index.html, http://www.pna-znp.org /pulaski1.htm.

Q: **Do you have any information about the history of the Spencer Theater that was across the street from Spencer Square in Rock Island?**

A: Not a lot, as it turns out. The only item we could find in our archives was this item from Sept. 3, 2002:

"50 years ago: Plans for a 124-car parking garage in downtown Rock Island were disclosed today by Robert D. Danico. The $105,000 project in the former Spencer Theater building, on the northeast corner of 19th Street and 2nd Avenue, will include all available area in the building with the exception of the corner area now occupied by the Lobby Tap."

We called on the memory of Bill McElwain, retired entertainment editor for The Dispatch and The Rock Island Argus. Mr. McElwain, in turn, tapped the recollections of another retired newsperson, Lois Schrage. Here's what he said:

"The Spencer Theater was on 2nd Avenue between 19th and 20th streets in downtown Rock Island — across from Spencer Square. Spencer Square was a beautiful, full-block park — trees, flowers and benches. There was a gazebo in the center of the square.

"Spencer Square was destroyed in the mid-1950s when the Rock Island Post Office and the federal courthouse were built on the site.

"The Spencer Theater was a small, second-run movie house. It ran double features, and admission was about 25 cents. The Spencer was never air-conditioned. It was in its hey day in the 1930s and 1940s. There's now a parking lot on the theater site.

"The Fort Theater (now Circa '21) on 3rd Avenue and 19th Street was the major theater in downtown Rock Island. It was a first-run movie house and was considered rather elegant.

"Also on 19th Street between 2nd and 3rd avenues was the Rocket Theater, named after the Rock Island Lines' Rocket, a passenger train which ran from Chicago to the Quad-Cities to Des Moines. The Rocket Theater later became the Capri. When it closed, there was an unsuccessful attempt to turn it into a nightclub. The building is now vacant.

"Incidentally, the Rocket was the only Quad City theater to install 'love seats' — seats which could accommodate two people.

"There was another second-run theater — the Riviera — a couple of blocks west of 19th Street.

"All of these downtown theaters began to fade when the mega-theater complexes and TV came into being. I have many happy memories of going to the movies in downtown Rock Island in the late 1930s, the 1940s and into the 1950s."

Q: I was just wondering if you could help me find out about a mayor of Davenport, Iowa? It would have been a man named Jebens? It's for school; my parents lived there years ago. Thank you, Jeff.

A: There have been two Jebenses who were Davenport mayor.

John H. Jebens Jr. served as mayor of Davenport from 1966 to 1972, after four terms as an alderman-at-large on the city council.

He also served on the Scott County Board of Supervisors and was a charter member of the Bi-State Metropolitan Planning Commission.

John H. Jebens
(Photo / file)

According to his obituary, Mr. Jebens operated the Black Hawk Printing Co. in Davenport and was active in Republican politics for most of his life. He died at age 56 on April 7, 1975, at his home on Arlington Avenue.

His father, John H. Jebens, also served as Davenport mayor, dying near the close of his second term in office.

Q: What happened to Harold's on the Rock? I used to go there a lot with my family for dinner, and my father and I used to go there a lot to just walk around and hang out by the river during the summer. Is there any way to actually visit the grounds again? I know the building is gone, but a walk down memory lane would be nice.

A: Harold's owners, Ken and Cheri Schloemer, finally got tired of the recurrent Rock River flooding that vexed the operation of the popular eatery and sold the 4.3 acre site to the Federal Emergency Management Agency.

FEMA turned the land over to the City of Moline.

The restaurant building was razed in 2000.

You certainly can visit the grounds. Moline has constructed a public boat-launch ramp on the site, and plans call for a playground to be added at some point.

Q: My great-great grandfather settled in Moline around 1850. I have a chair which my grandmother told me was made by him at a furniture factory on Arsenal Island. Was there indeed a factory there, and if so what was its name? (Incidentally, my aforementioned ancestor was Andrew Kittilsen, father of Col. Edward Kittilsen, once police chief in Rock Island, and whose statue is in Velie Park, Moline.)

A: Best we can do is to say there probably was a furniture factory on the island, and it probably was owned by David Sears, one of Moline's founders.

A 1996 Dispatch feature story recalling Mr. Sears said that, about 1845, he purchased land from the government on the island and on the adjoining mainland. "On his 57 acres, he built another mill, a warehouse, homes and another dam to power a lumber and furniture mill ..." But both an Army Corps of Engineers history of the island and Sears family records say Mr. Sears had just 37 acres on the island, leaving open the possibility that the furniture mill may have been on the mainland.

If it was on the island, the furniture factory likely was in operation for a maximum of 15 years or so. The government reclaimed all land on the island in 1865.

Mr. Sears, who had paid $1.25 an acre for his island land, or $46.25, according to family records, sold it back to the government for $145,175.

He used a portion of the money to buy land near Minneapolis, Minn., where he built, among other things, a sawmill and furniture factory.

The Sears family records referred to here can be found on the Web at http://www.genealogy.org/~lrsears/richard/d0008/g0000762.htm.

Q: When did the slide that went down into Rock River at Black Hawk State Park close? My father told me about it.

A: Marlene Gantt, author of the "Images of the Past" column that appears weekly in The Dispatch, fixed the date at "around 1925."

Quad-Citian Reva Winters, then 89, was quoted in a 2000 feature story about the Rock River as saying, "I went on the chute its last year, in 1923."

The "Shoot-the-Chute" slide was constructed in the 1890s and was part of an immense amusement park that also included a figure-8 roller coaster, hot-air ballon rides, shooting galleries, a 1,000-seat theater and a steady stream of speakers that included such luminaries as William Jennings Bryan and Gen. William Sherman.

Ms. Gantt, who had access to the memorabilia of developer James F. Lardner, found this contemporary description from a Clinton newspaper: "Here you start at 500 feet above the water on the inclined plane. After the descent begins, the speed increases and the wind whistles past like a tornado. You hang to the boat with one hand and grasp your hat with the other, and hold your breath to prevent it getting away from you. Then you strike the water and the boat gives a big jump, landing 25 to 50 feet distant right side up with care, and the boatman guides you back to the foot of the chute, where an electric motor hauls it and ocupants to the top."

The amusement park was developed and operated by local trolley-car company owners to promote weekend and evening use of the trolleys. They also promoted trolley parties featuring the park.

The July 4, 1896, festivities were reported to have drawn more than 15,000 people.

The park's popularity faded with the decline of trolley use; and local citizens in 1927 convinced the state to buy the site and return it to nature.

Q: On CNN today, I read the "crawl" at the bottom of the screen which said that on this date in 1885 the first successful appendectomy was performed in Davenport, Iowa. Where was this done, and by whom?

A: The appendectomy referred to was performed at Mercy Hospital by Dr. William Grant. The patient was Mary Gartside, 22, described as "a farm girl" and said to have recovered.

Whether Dr. Grant's appendectomy was actually the first one performed apparently is an issue. While we found many references to it in "timeline" and "today in history" Web pages, there also are other claimants.

A Frenchman, Claudius Aymand, also is credited in various places as having performed the first successful appendectomy. He is said to have done one in 1763 (1736 on some Web sites).

A Canadian doctor, Abraham Groves, performed the first successful appendectomy in North America on May 10, 1883, according to The Canadian Encyclopedia.

A British surgeon, Robert Lawson Tait, "the father of modern surgery," also is said to have performed the first recorded appendectomy, in 1880.

Q: Was there ever any industry on Campbell's Island?

A: Not that we've been able to find. The 250-acre island (in the Mississippi River off East Moline) is an unincorporated community in Rock Island County with a history that dates back to the War of 1812.

Its propensity to flood, and the limited access onto the island, probably have kept industry away.

The most well-known business on the island was the Campbell's Island Inn, later the Ship's Wheel and the Campbell's Island Marina, starting in

A 1948 photo of the Campbell's Island Inn, which later was known as the Ship's Wheel. (Photo / file)

the late 1940s. The vacant inn burned in 1979.

There are about 200 property owners on the island today. Various plans have been discussed involving recreational development on the island but nothing is under way. Many residents have been opposed to development or annexation to the city of East Moline.

Q: Did I read somewhere that the first neon sign ever was lit in Moline?

A: Don't know if you read that or not, but if you did you were apparently getting bad information.

According to Inventors World Magazine, "A public display of the first neon light was by Claude in December 1910."

A history of neon on the Neonworks of Cincinnati Web site says inventor Georges Claude did that 1910 display at the Grand Palais in Paris.

The first neon light in America? At a Packard automobile dealership in Los Angeles, according to the Neonworks history.

Q: **A number of relics were found at the Cook Farm Mounds in Davenport. Are these relics in the collection at the Putnum Museum in Davenport? Where was the Cook Farm located? The items were taken to the Smithsonian and were supposedly a hoax. Can you find more information on this subject?**

A: The story of the relics found at Cook Farm Mounds is fascinating.

The relics, a number of pipes and several stone tablets containing what appeared to be symbolic writings and pictures, were widely hailed as one of the great archaeological discoveries of all time after they were found in 1874-1878.

They were said to prove that some Middle Eastern or North African people had lived in the area in pre-historic times, and carried great weight in what was then one of the great debates among archaeologists. But doubters existed, and the relics were at the center of an international controversy that raged for 40 years in professional journals and which, to at least some small degree, continues today.

The dispute eventually split the Davenport Academy of Natural Sciences, leading to the forced ouster of some of its founding members who contended the relics had been planted. Officials at the Smithsonian Institute, whose preliminary examination of the relics was presented as validating the authenticity of the items, soon became the most prominent critics of the find.

Chief among the defenders of the relics was Charles Putnam, a prominent Davenport attorney whose family name the Putnam Museum bears.

There's a considerable amount of information about the relics on the Web, but we're indebted to Eunice J. Schlichting, chief curator at the Putnam, for guiding us to *The Davenport Conspiracy Revisited*, a 1991 book by former Iowa state archaeologist Marshall McKusick. She said Mr. McKusick's book is considered "the definitive work" on the controversy and that the museum "concurs with (his) conclusion that the tablets are fakes."

The book is out of print, but most public libraries in the Quad-Cities have a copy. In it, Mr. McKusick, who conducted extensive research into primary sources and who examined the items, concludes persuasively that the relics were planted in the mounds, probably by members of the Davenport academy, either as a joke on the Rev. Jacob Gass or as an attempt to embarass him. The reverend, an enthusiastic but amateur seeker after relics in the mounds that dotted the area, apparently was an abrasive man with enemies in the academy.

Mr. McKusick says that Rev. Gass, who turned the items over to the academy without making any claim as to what they were, probably did not realize for several years that he had been duped. In the meantime, the early, seeming endorsement of authenticity by the Smithsonian led many members of the Davenport academy and other, more prominent, authorities in the field to believe fiercely that the relics were a critically important find.

Ms. Schlichting reports "the Davenport Tablets and several related fraudulent pipes are currently on display at the Museum."

She notes, too, that the museum has a collection of authentic relics taken from the Cook Farm Mounds. The mounds, Mr. McKusick says in his book, yielded many items of genuine archaeological value, many of them found by Rev. Gass in hurried, unscientific excavations.

Mr. McKusick, in the 1991 book, pinpoints the mounds' location as being "covered by the building of the Thompson-Hayward Chemical Company, 2040 W. River St."

Charles Putnam's 1885 defense of the relics and the integrity of the Davenport Academy is entitled *Elephant Pipes and Inscribed Tablets.*

The Davenport Public Libary has two copies in its non-circulating collection.

Also of interest is a chapter in Harry E. Downer's 1912 *History of Davenport and Scott County, Iowa.* It can be found at http://www.celticcousins.net/scott/Chapter2.html.

Q: I have heard that Abraham Lincoln stayed in these parts sometime during the time he was in the Army. Is that true? If so, where?

A: The first question is easy: Yes, Lincoln stayed in these parts while serving in the Illinois Militia in 1832, during the Black Hawk War.

Where he stayed, precisely, is a more difficult, perhaps even impossible, question to answer. "The mouth of Rock River" is the best we could find.

That's from Frank E. Stevens' 1903 book, "The Black Hawk War." It contains a detailed record of Lincoln's service, along with evaulations of the various tales and stories told about the future president's days in the militia.

Thanks to the Illinois Historical Digitization Projects and Northern Illinois University Libraries, much of Mr. Stevens' work can be found online. The portion related to Lincoln's services is at http://lincoln.lib.niu.edu/cgi-bin/getobject_?c.1580:42./lib35/artfl1/databases/sources/IMAGE.

Q: When I was in elementary school in Davenport in the early 1960s, my mom and I would take the bus up to Palmer College to visit Little Bit of Heaven. I remember all the truly exotic statues and art work. Is it still there and available for public viewing? I now live in Michigan and would like to know if I could take my adult daughter to see these treasures.

A: Sorry, but "A Little Bit O' Heaven" ceased to exist in 1982.

Created in 1924 by Palmer College of Chiropractic founder B. J. Palmer, the rock and sculpture garden/greenhouse drew more than 2 million people over the years, according to "Davenport — a Pictorial History."

The entrance to A Little Bit O' Heaven.
(Photo / file)

Interest dwindled in the 1970s, and the site was open only irregularly.

A Palmer College spokeswoman said the end came in the winter of 1982, when power to the area was inadvertently left off and the resulting freeze heavily damaged the area. The college chose to demolish the garden rather than undertake costly repairs.

Q: **I was surfing the net recently, and ... saw a reference to a firm called Rock Island Plow. I've had no luck finding anything about this firm other than one site on the net which had pictures of a Rock Island Plow restored engine. Can you tell me if this was a one-time business of the Quad-Cities and just where was it located?**

A: The Rock Island Plow Co., headquartered in Rock Island, was once a major farm-implement manufacturer with a worldwide business. Dating to the 1850s, Rock Island Plow's plant was at 2nd Avenue and 6th Street. It was sold to J.I. Case Co., in 1937 and continued operations until Case closed the 26-acre site in 1988.

An interesting sidelight is that Rock Island Plow Co. constructed the building in Dallas, Tex., that was known as the Texas School Book Depository in 1963, when Lee Harvey Oswald shot President John Kennedy from the sixth floor.

Q: **I understand that Credit Island was the site of a battle in the War of 1812. U.S. troops were led by Zachary Taylor, who later became president. But I have** **been having difficulty finding details about the battle, its specific location, troop movements, number of casualties, any first hand accounts, etc.**

A: The battle of Credit Island was fought Sept. 6, 1814, between a force of 340 Americans under the command of Maj. Zachary Taylor and a force of approximately 1,000 Indians, one of whom was the Sauk war leader Black Hawk. The Indians were assisted by 30 British soldiers under the command of Lt. Duncan Graham.

The mission of the Taylor expedition, dispatched from St. Louis, was to retaliate against Indians in the Rock Island area for their deadly attack in July, 1814, on a force commanded by Lt. John Campbell (after whom Campbell's Island off East Moline — the site of the attack — is named).

The Americans fought primarily from the boats on which they were traveling up the Mississippi. The British-Indian force fought from Credit Island and both sides of the river. The Americans, hampered by their cumbersome boats and unfavorable winds, withdrew down-river after several hours of fighting. Maj. Taylor reported he had 11 men badly wounded, three mortally. Lt. Graham said that "not a man was hurt" on the British side.

The above information is based primarily upon the after-action reports filed with their respective commanders by Maj. Taylor and Lt. Graham. We found those on the Celtic Cousins Web site. The pertinent page (http://www.celticcousins.net/scott/chapter5.html) also contains accounts of other key events in relations between whites and Indians in the

Rock Island area, including a description of the much-bloodier battle of Campbell's Island.

Q: Whose skeleton used to hang in the Hauberg Museum at Black Hawk State Park, and what happened to it?

A: Although it's officially the Hauberg *Indian* Museum, it was not the skeleton of a Native American. The museum housed the bones of a notorious white man, John Long, one of the killers hanged in Rock Island on Oct. 29, 1845, for the murder of Col. George Davenport.

After the execution, Long's body was given to Dr. P.P. Gregg for study. Dr. Gregg kept Long's skeleton on display in his office at the Rock Island Arsenal hospital for years. At some point, Long's skeleton lost its notoriety and didn't resurface until 1940, when it was mailed to the Rock Island County Historical Society by a Chicago doctor who received the gruesome legacy from Dr. Gregg's widow.

Long's remains found a home for many years in a display case at the Rock Island County Courthouse until his bones were transferred to the Hauberg Indian Museum, where they were displayed until about 1975. He was buried Sept. 14, 1978, but not until the county coroner issued a death certificate to prove he was legally dead!

Although Long's body may not have always been treated with respect, it was put to rest properly. "He got a pretty good burial; I think he had two ministers. It wasn't too bad for the scoundrel that he was," said Greg Vogele of Chippiannock Cemetery in 1978.

An interesting side note to the story is that Long was buried in the little-known Dickson Cemetery at Black Hawk State Historic Site, Rock Island.

Dickson (or Pioneer Cemetery) was the first non-Indian burial site in Rock Island and was sometimes used as a paupers' graveyard. It covers about two acres in the northwest corner of the site. The first graves date to the 1850s. The state acquired the cemetery in 1942, and John Long is the only person buried there since then. His grave is unmarked.

Q: I have seen the Warner Castle up in Orion. Can anyone give me some background information about the castle?

A: Warner Castle, located about five miles north of Orion, Ill., was built in 1895 by Wilder Williston Warner (1828-1899).

Warner Castle ... the family called it 'The Oaks.' (Photo / file)

Warner was the son of a Boston doctor. He arrived in Rock Island in 1849 and took a job as a teacher there and later in Andover. After a few years he took his savings and went into farming. His first land purchase in northwest Henry County became the basis for the new town of Warner (some called it Warner Station), which flourished as a railroad stop and commerce center for many years, but died in the Great Depression.

At any rate, Warner's fortunes were good, and he ended up with about 1,500 acres, a grain business and several related enterprises.

He was a world traveler and evidently had a fascination with castles, so he collected ideas on his travels for his own. It took five years and $80,000 to build the 17-room Warner Castle with sandstone from Cleveland Quarry near Colona. (The Rock Island County Courthouse and some Arsenal buildings are made of the same stone.) The castle has 12-foot ceilings, and three huge granite-and-marble fireplaces.

The castle has three floors and its 60-foot tower offers an impressive view of the countryside. Some say that on a clear day you can see Orion from it.

The castle remained in the family until Warner's son, Lawrence, died in 1947.

According to an interview when he was 84 years old, Lawrence said the family never referred to their home as Warner Castle, but preferred to call it "The Oaks." The castle is included in the Illinois Historic Landmark Survey.

Q: A Count Theodor Dembinski is buried in the old city cemetery at the foot of Division Street in Davenport. Why? Who was he?

A: The count is a mystery. The reference librarians at the Davenport Public Library searched everything they could think of, and they did confirm that he's buried here, but why is a mystery.

He died Nov. 14, 1854, in St. Louis. That much is confirmed by the cemetery records. But census records, property records and tax records don't show him. Nor do the newspaper obits from that period.

We suspect that he was buried in Davenport because he had some family ties here. According to genealogical records of the Rombauer families (http://web.utk.edu/~arombaue/famhist.html#), the count's widow, Emilie Marie Sophie Hogl, married into another family with extensive contacts in St. Louis and Davenport.

Thanks to everyone who helped us look for info.

Q: When was the last public hanging done in the Q-C area? I have heard from other people that crowds of people in the early years would come from miles around with their picnic baskets to watch the event of the day.

A: Members of the Rock Island County Historical Society graciously did some research. The results:

"We found information on the Davenport case, of course, and also on the David Stoddard hanging on July 13, 1855. 'It was public and attracted a large crowd.'

"Samuel Ingram was hanged on July 3, 1857, on the same scaffold at the same spot.

"We found references to the Heilwagon hanging on March 24, 1883, called the 'first private execution in Rock Island County,' which was performed before an audience of about 125 persons.

"Those who had tickets struggled with those who did not.

"A couple of us here think that there was a hanging in Rock Island County in the early 20th century, around 1910 or so, but it was probably private. Unfortunately, we just can't find any information to support that.

"And, if you are including the entire Quad-Cities area, we don't have much information on Scott County. So, it seems that the last public hanging in Rock Island County may have been the Ingram case. We just can't be certain about this."

A reader adds: "About the public hanging: A former neighbor of mine was some kind of a deputy, and he used to talk about it. He died the same day JFK died. I did some research at the Rock Island Public Library and came across microfilmed articles in The Argus about a black man who murdered a white man. The killer was hanged, and this took place, I think, around 1917-1918. I can remember seeing articles about World War I (only it wasn't called that at the time as no one knew there was going to be a World War II).

"I used to know the names of the killer and victim, but I just don't remember what they are ... I believe the man who was hanged was buried in a Davenport cemetery."

Q: During my youth, many of us played on the island next to the RI Arsenal. It was called Sullivan's Slough or just the slough. There are remnants of many buildings on the island, replete with tunnels and other underground corridors. Can you tell us (A) what industry was once there, and (B) what the real name of the island is, and (C) who owns

This undated aerial photo of Sylvan Island shows the steel plant that once operated there. The plant, closed in 1956, has long been demolished, though some of the foundation is incorporated into the walking paths criss-crossing Sylvan Island Park. (Photo/ file)

it — the Army or the city of Rock Island?

A: To begin with, it is Sylvan Island and Sylvan Slough (not Sullivan's).

Once a small peninsula, the 38 acres became an island in 1871 when a millrace was cut through the peninsula's base as part of a water-power project jointly developed by the federal government and the Moline Water Power Co.

The island was leased to the Sylvan Steel Co. in 1894, and was the site of a steel plant, later operated by Republic Steel Co., until 1956. In 1966 the city of Moline acquired the island as a site for a park.

Progress on the park was slow but, with strong support from a group calling itself the Sylvan Island Dreamers, much has been accomplished. There is an open-air welcome center, overlooks, fishing piers, picnic tables, and strategically placed benches scattered along the network of walking paths on the island.

Q: Has there ever been a Republican mayor of the city of East Moline?

A: We handed this question off to Don Jacobs, a former East Moline alderman, current Rock Island County board member, and a walking encyclopedia of local politics.

His answer: Yes and no.

Mr. Jacobs said no one was ever elected mayor of East Moline as a Republican although several people elected as independents decades ago were really Republicans. He said these included Charlie Carpentier, who

later was elected Illlinois Secretary of State as a Republican.

If anyone has additional information, please share it.

A reader adds: "I believe John Siefken was a Republican when he served as East Moline mayor back in the 1930s."

Another says: "I believe that Ray Klingbiel was mayor of East Moline and was also a Republican."

Q: I'm 15 years old and I have an ongoing debate with my father. He says that the I-74 bridge was never a toll bridge. However, my teachers all say that it was. Could you by any chance help me on this?

A: Your teachers are right. In this photo, Dave Power of Rock Island is shaking hands with toll-taker Leo Jipp of Bettendorf. Mr. Power had just paid the last toll, at noon on Dec. 31, 1969. That day the Davenport Bridge Commission turned the bridge over to the states of Iowa and Illinois.

W.P. Bettendorf proposed a Bettendorf-to-Moline bridge in the early 1900s. The first two-lane Moline-to-Bettendorf bridge, then called the Memorial Bridge, opened in 1935, and today this bridge carries southbound I-74 traffic. Because of demand on that bridge, a virtually identical span was completed in 1959, which now carries northbound traffic. The twin spans were upgraded to carry Interstate traffic in the mid-1970s.

In 1998, I-74 was carrying nearly 70,000 vehicles daily.

Q: What is the oldest building in the Quad-Cities?

A: We thought the oldest structure had to be the Col. Davenport House on Arsenal Island. The house, which is open to the public much of the year, was built by the prominent pioneer George Davenport in 1833-36.

However, Marcia Wetzel, president of the Davenport House Historical Foundation, says that while the Davenport House is the oldest residence in the Quad-Cities, it may not be the oldest building.

One of George Davenport's sons put up a "claim house" sometime before the Davenport House was built. In those days, if you wanted to stake claim to a piece of property, you put some kind of structure on it, even if you didn't live in it (which he did not). Thus the name "Claim House."

According to some sources, the Claim House's location was near present-day Bettendorf, and it was not only the first building in the Quad-Cities area, but was the first house built west of the Mississippi River. The Claim House has been moved several times and is a private residence today.

Q: I have heard that Edgar Allen Poe is buried in a cemetery in Davenport. Is this true?

A: No. According to his biography at the Poe Museum in Richmond, Va., "The circumstances of Poe's death remain a mystery. After a visit to Norfolk and Richmond for lectures, he was found in Baltimore in a pitiable condition and taken unconscious to a hospital where he died on Sunday, October 7, 1849. He was buried in the yard of Westminster Presbyterian Church in Baltimore, Maryland."

You may have been thinking of a different author. Francis Jeffrey Dickens, son of British novelist Charles Dickens, is buried on the east side of Riverside Cemetery, 27th Street and 5th Avenue, Moline. Mr. Dickens died June 11, 1886, while visiting in Moline.

One reader e-mailed us to say that Poe died from rabies. We hadn't heard this, so we contacted the Poe Museum, and this is what they said:

"Please see John Evangelist Walsh's book *Midnight Dreary, The Mysterious Death of Edgar Allan Poe*. There are many theories on the cause of Poe's death. The rabies theory is in Vol. 45 No. 9 of the September 1996 *Maryland Medical Journal*. Good luck in your studies."

Q: I was told the Wittenmyer Youth Center in Davenport used to be a Civil War veterans' home. Is this true?

A: Not quite, though the site does have a couple of Civil War connections. First, there was a training camp for soldiers bound for Civil War battlefields. Then, in 1865, shortly after the war ended, the state opened the Iowa Soldiers' Orphans Home to house and educate children orphaned by the war.

The home continued to care for orphans long after those left parentless by the Civil War were grown and gone. The name was changed to in 1949 to honor Annie Wittenmyer, a reformer and worker for the Iowa Orphans' Home Association.

The orphange was closed in the late 1960s, and the campus now houses a variety of community organizations.

Q: **I understand Abraham Lincoln visited Rock Island in 1857 as a lawyer defending the owners of a bridge which had been struck by the Effie Afton. Was this the first bridge across the Mississippi? Where was this bridge? Where did Lincoln stay? Are there any other connections between the Quad-Cities and Illinois' most famous resident?**

A: The bridge struck by the Effie Afton, near the site of today's Government Bridge, was indeed the first across the Mississippi. The first train crossed April 22, 1856. Barely two weeks later, on May 6, the Effie Afton passed through the swing span, then drifted back into the bridge, catching it on fire.

Lincoln represented the railroad interests in the ensuing legal battle with riverboat interests. A court ordered the bridge removed, but appeals carried the matter before the U. S. Supreme Court, which decided in 1862 in *Hurd v. Rock Island Bridge Co.* that railroads have the right to bridge navigable streams.

Q: **I have discovered my great-great grandmother was supposedly buried in a cemetery in Black Hawk State Park, now Black Hawk Historical Site. I seem to have read about a cemetery located there in the Dispatch a couple of years ago. Was or is there a cemetery in The park? Does anyone know of its location?**

A: Yes, there is a cemetery in Black Hawk State Historic Site. Called the Dickson Pioneer Cemetery, it covers about two acres in the northwest corner of the site. Beth Stewart, of the historic site museum, said the first graves in the cemetery date to the 1850s, and that it was once used as a paupers' graveyard.

She said the state acquired the cemetery in 1942. The only burial there since came Sept. 14, 1978, when the skeleton of John Long was interred there after having spent 133 years in the Rock Island County Court House, where it had once been displayed in a glass case. Long was hanged in Rock Island on Oct. 29, 1845, for his part in the murder of Col. George Davenport on July 4 of that year.

Q: **I would like to know, using landmarks that we recognize today, where exactly was the infamous John Looney's son Connor and several of his henchman shot and killed? I ask that because my grandmother would tell me that she went to school with Connor Looney and the gunfight happened in front of my great-grandfather's lunch wagon,**

approximately where the Sheraton stands today.

A: According to stories in our newspaper archives, Connor Looney was gunned down Oct. 6, 1922, outside the Sherman Hotel in Rock Island, which stood where the Four Points is today. There is no reference to whether it was the 2nd Avenue, 3rd Avenue, or 17th Street side — although some say that it was on 17th Street near where Steve's Old Time stands today.

It was described as the greatest gunfight of the era with more than 40 shots fired.

Q: Did the old football team called the Rock Island Independents wear an Indian Head logo on their jerseys? Also, is there a photo of Jim Thorpe when he played for them?

A: We haven't been able to find an answer to your first question, but the accompanying photo may be of Thorpe in an Independents uniform. We found it in our files. It came from United Press International to go with a 1975 story about the effort to get the International Olympics Committee to restore the medals Thorpe won in 1912, but which were later taken away when it was discovered he had played professional minor league baseball

Jim Thorpe

prior to the 1912 Games. UPI identified it as a 1925 photo, and Thorpe played for the Independents that year.

In the background of the more detailed UPI photo, the words "Apper Bros." can be seen on what appears to be an advertising sign. If there was an "Apper Bros." company in Rock Island in 1925, the photo would almost certainly be of Thorpe in an Independents uniform, but we've been unable to determine if such a company existed.

Perhaps one of our readers will recall whether there was an Indian Head logo on the uniforms, or whether there was an "Apper Bros." in Rock Island.

The Independents were one of the original National Football League teams.

Incidentally, the IOC in 1982 — 29 years after Thorpe's death — restored the gold medals he won in the decathlon and pentathlon in the 1912 games in Stockholm, Sweden.

Thorpe, a member of the Sac-Fox tribe, is still considered by many to be the greatest athlete of all time. In addition to his Olympics triumphs, he played both pro football and major league baseball.

Q: Was there ever an NBA team located in the Quad-Cities? Someone told me that one used to play at Warton Field house.

A: Yes. The Tri-City Blackhawks were among the charter teams when the National Basketball Association was formed in 1949. They did play at Wharton Field House in Moline.

The '49-50 season feaured Arnold "Red" Auerbach as coach and future hall-of-famer Bob Cousy among the players. Auerbach left after the season to take over as coach of the Boston Celtics. The Blackhawks traded Cousy to the Chicago Stags, but they folded before the next season started and Cousy moved on to Boston, where he has a vital part of the dynasty Auerbach built there. The Blackhawks lasted only through the '50-51 season, after which they moved to Milwaukee and were renamed the Hawks. After the '54-55 season the Hawks moved to St. Louis, where they played through '67-68. They moved again, to Atlanta, where they live on as the Atlanta Hawks.

A reader adds: "Re: the Tri-City Blackhawks, there is a very large picture of the team located at the Wunder Y Tap, 2316 16th St., Moline."

Another says: "I believe that the Tri-City Blackhawks moved to the Tri-Cities from Buffalo, N.Y., where they played under the name of the Buffalo Bisons, in 1946. I remember that they wore the old Buffalo uniforms for the first few games that they played in Wharton Fieldhouse. I also recall that the name of the league was the National Basketball League, which later merged, in 1949, with the Basketball Association of America to become the National Basketball Association. The original Blackhawks team included such stars-of-the-day as Don Otten, Billy Hassett, Joe Camic, "Whitey" Von Nieda, "Pop" Gates (Hall Of Famer) and Don Ray and later picked-up University Of Illinois "Whiz Kids," Gene Vance and "Dike" Eddleman and University of Iowa All-American, Murray Wier."

Rex watches forever over the graves of the Dimick children in Rock Island's Chippiannock Cemetery. (Photo / file)

of his faithful Newfoundland next to the graves of his children. What cemetery was the statue placed in, and is it still there?

A: The cemetery is Chippiannock in Rock Island and, yes, the statue is still there.

The children were Josie and Eddie Dimick. Josie, 9, and Eddie, 5, both died of diptheria Oct. 22, 1878.

The story is that the family's Newfoundland, believed to have been named Rex, would follow the children's parents when they visited the grave.

Eventually, the dog began going to the cemetery on his own and in time began spending every day, from sunrise to sunset, at the grave. When he died, the family commissioned the statue and placed it near the tombstone.

Q: A "Today in History" on Quad-Cities Online for 125 years ago said a man installed a statue

Q: Whatever happened to our hometown hero John Baker? I remember the Medal of Honor winner when he returned home

from Vietnam. I was at the parade held in his honor.

A: John F. Baker Jr., as of late 2004, is alive and living in Columbia, S.C., where he works at a Veterans' Affairs hospital.

Mr. Baker was just 21 when he participated in a particularly savage jungle fight in Vietnam. Besides killing several snipers firing on the Americans, he also dragged several wounded comrades to safety. His actions won him a Medal of Honor, which was presented him by President Lyndon Johnson in a White House ceremony.

Here's the text of the citation:

"The President of the United States in the name of The Congress takes pleasure in presenting the Medal of Honor to BAKER, JOHN F., JR.

John Baker

Rank and organization: Sergeant (then Pfc.), U.S. Army, Company A, 2d Battalion, 27th Infantry, 25th Infantry Division. Place and date: Republic of Vietnam, 5 November 1966. Entered service at: Moline, Ill. Born: 30 October 1945, Davenport, Iowa.

"Citation: For conspicuous gallantry and intrepidity in action at the risk of his life above and beyond the call of duty. En route to assist another unit that was engaged with the enemy, Company A came under intense enemy fire and the lead man was killed instantly. Sgt. Baker immediately moved to the head of the column and together with another soldier knocked out 2 enemy bunkers.

"When his comrade was mortally wounded, Sgt. Baker, spotting 4 Viet Cong snipers, killed all of them, evacuated the fallen soldier and returned to lead repeated assaults against the enemy positions, killing several more Viet Cong. Moving to attack 2 additional enemy bunkers, he and another soldier drew intense enemy fire and Sgt. Baker was blown from his feet by an enemy grenade. He quickly recovered and single-handedly destroyed 1 bunker before the other soldier was wounded. Seizing his fallen comrade's machinegun, Sgt. Baker charged through the deadly fusillade to silence the other bunker. He evacuated his comrade, replenished his ammunition and returned to the forefront to brave the enemy fire and continue the fight. When the forward element was ordered to withdraw, he carried 1 wounded man to the rear. As he returned to evacuate another soldier, he was taken under fire by snipers, but raced beyond the friendly troops to attack and kill the snipers. After evacuating the wounded man, he returned to cover the deployment of the unit.

"His ammunition now exhausted, he dragged 2 more of his fallen comrades to the rear. Sgt. Baker's selfless heroism, indomitable fighting spirit, and extraordinary gallantry were directly responsible for saving the lives of several of his comrades, and inflicting serious damage on the enemy. His acts were in keeping with the highest traditions of the U.S. Army and reflect great credit upon himself and the Armed Forces of his country."

There was indeed a parade in his honor in Moline when he returned home.

Quad-Citians also chipped in to build him a new house.

Mr. Baker retired from the Army as a master sergeant in 1989.

In 2004, former classmates at Moline High School initiated an effort to include him in the school's Hall of Honor, which recognizes former students who particularly distinguish themselves. The committee which controls the Hall of Honor refused to do so, on the grounds that Mr. Baker had not graduated, which is a condition for inclusion.

In the face of a community outcry, the school included a plaque recognizing Mr. Baker on a wall that previously inluded only a general recognition of all MHS students who've served in the Armed Forces.

Rock Island firefights confer outside the ice-covered ruins of the Rock Island Labor Temple Dec. 19, 1980. (Photo / file)

The remains of the building were demolished the following spring.

Q: **What year was the fire that destroyed the Labor Temple in Rock Island?**

A: That would be 1980; the night of Dec. 18-19, to be precise.

The 86-year-old building at 2100 3rd Ave., on the National Historic Register, housed a tavern on the first floor and a number of labor union offices on its upper two floors. Designed by George P. Staduhar, an early architect responsible for a number of other prominent Rock Island buildings, the building was gutted by the fire. Winds up to 40 miles per hour and temperatures that dropped into the single digits hampered firefighters and turned the entire area into an ice-covered maze.

The exact cause of the fire was never determined, though officials speculated a problem in the electrical system, probably in the northeast corner of the second floor, sparked the blaze.

Q: **I was driving on Highway 34 in Galesburg and noticed a sign for the Ronald Reagan Trail. What is the trail about and what is the route?**

A: The "Ronald Reagan Trail" was created by the Illinois General Assembly in 1999 to celebrate "the hometown values and heritage of our 40th President."

The trail comprises a loop from Princeton to Galesburg to Peoria, with spurs to Monmouth, Eureka, Tampico and Dixon. Mr. Reagan, of course, was born in Tampico and spent some of his early years in Galeburg and Monmouth before moving to Dixon, which he considered his hometown. He went to college in Eureka.

For a map of the trail and more information about Reagan connections along its route, visit The Ronald Reagan Trail Web site: http://www.ronaldreagantrail.net/.

A Few Favorite Foods

Q: **Would anyone out there have the recipe for the old Plantation salad which was served at the Plantation Restaurant in the 1960s?**

A: There's only one good source for this kind of question, and that's Liz Meegan, author of the "Curious Cook" column for The Dispatch and The Rock Island Argus.

"I really don't think anyone has the *official* version, and I'll tell you why," she said. "A number of years ago, Curious Cook received that same request for the Plantation Salad. After publishing the request, Curious Cook received many, many recipes, all of them similar and all claiming to be 'the recipe.' Well, after publication of all those recipes, one of the former owners of The Plantation called me and said, 'All very interesting, Liz, but none of them is the recipe'!"

That said, Mrs. Meegan kindly went through her files back to 1983 and sent us the Plantation Salad "wannabe" recipes that follow.

The Curious Cook, Feb. 16, 1983

It's amazing how many versions The Curious Cook has received of "authentic" Plantation Dressing. The dressing certainly must be the most popular — the all-time favorite — of restaurant "house dressings" in the Quad City area.

I'm sure the request brings back many happy memories for readers who so much enjoyed dining at The Plantation in Moline.

I'm going to share the letters and notes I received from area cooks who sent in recipes for the dressing. I think you'll enjoy reading them and will identify with them. Some of the directions of the "authentic" recipes differ, so I shall include the variations.

There seem to be quite a few "real things." And too, some recipes were more complete than others because they include exact sizes for bottles.

As you probably already know, Quad-Citians simply loved that garlicky house dressing at The Plantation. I do not know whether or not owners Al Johnson, Dave Koenig and Gary Huysman and general manager Wes Llewellyn plan to feature the dressing when they open W.L. Velie's this spring. I would like to suggest they do so. No, I urge them, to put the Plantation Dressing on the menu.

Remodeling in The Plantation, the old W.L. Velie mansion, began in January, and Quad-Citians are awaiting announcement of the reopening date.

The new name reflects, the history of the magnificent mansion which was built by W.L. Velie on 7th St. near Black Hawk Road. Velie, a Moliner, designed and manufactured the famous Velie automobile and later the Monocoupe airplane.

If there's any doubt in your mind about the popularity of The Plantation through many years, or its house dressing, read on.

We'll start with an interesting letter from Mrs. H.H. of Coal Valley. She captures the feeling the public has about Plantation house dressing.

"I'm positive I have the original Plantation Dressing (or a reasonable facsimile.) I moved to the Quad-Cities as a bride in 1948 and shortly thereafter started working at the Rock Island Arsenal.

"Whenever an occasion warranted, the girls in our office going out to eat for a special treat, The Plantation was the 'in' place at that time, and the main reason for going there was the salad dressing. Even the most fastidious couldn't resist the garlic dressing and we all left the place with the worst garlic breath. But it was worth it.

"Then one day, someone brought the recipe to the office and very surreptitiously passed it around for us to copy — with the reminder that it had been 'sneaked' out, etc. (At that time, you could buy the bottled dressing from The Plantation.)

"But with all that clandestine operation, it had to be the one. Because I had eaten so much of it, when I started making my own I could account for every ingredient. I'm sure the eggs, A-1 sauce, ketchup, mustard, garlic oil or garlic salt are the result of people altering or adding to the recipe. (This is bound to happen over the years, especially when people try to remember ingredients or guess at them.)

"Not only was I sure of it because of the taste, but I knew the people well enough who passed the recipe around that I believed them when they said it was the 'real' one.

"After all these years it doesn't matter who divulged a supposedly secret recipe, but I felt at the time that I was the proud possessor of THE RECIPE for the famous Plantation house dressing. And I still feel the same about it after 30 years. It is one of my most treasured recipes, not only because it is so good, but it represents an era in the history of the Plantation that now is just a memory.

"I'm sure this is the recipe Mrs. D.E.E. of Moline is looking for."

Plantation Dressing

1 pint Hellman's mayonnaise
1 cup Kraft French dressing (thin dressing)
2 teaspoons anchovy paste, optional
2 buds garlic, grated
1 can Parmesan cheese
Melba toast

Toss lettuce with dressing. Add Melba toast last.

Important note: Use nothing but Hellman's and Kraft French dressing (the thin dressing). Be sure to use the Kraft thin dressing. NO SUBSTITUTIONS. —**Mrs. H.H. of Coal Valley**

Plantation Salad Dressing

"I am responding to the request for 'Plantation-style Dressing.' However, the recipe does not include all of the ingredients as suggested by Mrs. D.E.E. of Moline," writes S.O. of Moline.

Here's S.O.'s version. She in turn attributes it to a Mrs. Ivan Graham, Davenport, Iowa, in "Jim Lloyd's Best of the Open Line Cookbook, 1969."
1 pint mayonnaise
½ bottle creamy French dressing
1 can grated Romano cheese
2 chopped garlic cloves
½ tube anchovy paste
Melba toast
Grated Parmesan cheese

Mix all ingredients — except Melba toast and grated cheese — in blender.

Cover and store dressing in refrigerator. Use dressing on mixed lettuce, radishes and tomatoes. — *S.O. of Moline*

M.H. of Moline has a recipe that includes garlic powder.
1 pint real mayonnaise
1 small bottle homogenized French dressing — orange
2 teaspoons garlic powder
1 small can of Parmesan cheese
2 teaspoons anchovy paste

Mix well and store in a covered jar in refrigerator. — *M.H. of Moline*

S.G. of East Moline says she worked at The Plantation Club for a short time.

Here's her version, which includes onion!
1 pint mayonnaise (Hellmann's)

*1 battle Kraft orange French dressing,
small size*
2 teaspoons anchovy paste
2 cloves garlic, crushed through a press
½ medium-size onion, chopped
1 small can grated Parmesan cheese

Combine all ingredients; mix well with a blender. Store in glass jar — keeps. — *S.G. of East Moline*

"This is the real dressing from The Plantation," writes B.G. of Moline. "I used to buy it in Rock Island at Bogart's years ago. He sold all the Plantation things."

1 quart Hellman's mayonnaise
½ pint Kraft (yellow) French dressing
*Large can of grated cheese (Romano or
Parmesan)*
1 tablespoon anchovy paste
1 clove garlic, crushed

Combine all ingredients but DO NOT COOK. "This is really good." — *B.G. of Moline*

The Curious Cook, Feb. 23, 1983

"Needless to say, I was, just delighted to read the response to my request for the Plantation Dressing from your thoughtful readers," writes Mrs. D.E.E. of Moline. "I was amazed at the difference in ingredients I have been working with and the correct ones. I have copied each and every recipe and propose to try them all one after the other, VERY soon. They sound delicious! Many thanks to you and your contributors." — *Mrs. D.E.E. of Moline*

Plantation dressings

Although the subject of The Plantation's famous house dressing was covered extensively in last week's column, N.B. of Moline has a completely different version which certainly deserves mention.

The request for the "real" house dressing which made the lettuce salad at The Plantation restaurant in Moline famous throughout the community, drew quite a response from area cooks. Indeed, the number of "authentic" versions which arrived in The Curious Cook's mail must have amused our readers. The contributors are a good example of how recipes change, or are changed, as they are shared.

N.B. sent us two recipes, one being identical to the combination of Hellmann's mayonnaise, Kraft French dressing, anchovy paste and minced garlic buds featured in last week's Taste section. Cooks generally seem to agree on that particular combination as the "true recipe."

Anyone who enjoyed The Plantation salad remembers not only how good it was but how garlicky it was. An usher at Sunday morning services at a Moline church once told me he always knew who had been at The Plantation on Saturday night!

The second recipe for the Plantation-Style Dressing submitted by N.B. is just a bit more involved than those published last week and it differs considerably from those recipes.

Plantation-style Dressing

1 pint Wesson oil
4 to 5 garlic buds
1 egg, well beaten
1 teaspoon salt
2 teaspoons sugar
1 teaspoon dry mustard
2 tablespoons vinegar
1 teaspoon Worcestershire sauce
Dash of A-1 sauce
Dash of Tabasco sauce
2 tablespoons ketchup
Parmesan cheese
Lettuce, torn in pieces
Melba toast

Combine Wesson oil and garlic buds. Let marinate for about 2 or 3 weeks!

When ready to prepare dressing, beat egg well. Add salt, sugar and mustard. Beat this together well. Then add Wesson oil SLOWLY. Lastly add vinegar, Worcestershire, A-1 and Tabasco sauces and ketchup. Pour Parmesan cheese over lettuce and add dressing. Melba toast also may be added. — *N.B. of Moline*

Q: **Here's a silly one for ya. How do you hard-boil an egg so the shell comes off easy every time? I use one of those egg timers that go in the water with the eggs and cool them after the boil, but sometimes the shell is hard to get off and removes some of the whites with it.**

A: It's not a silly question. You've no doubt noticed that if you're making egg salad, the shells just slide off, but it you're making deviled eggs, the eggs end up looking as though you sandblasted the shell off!

First rule: Use eggs that are 7-10 days old. If you don't know how old they are, you can test them: Put the egg in a bowl of water. If it sits on the bottom of the bowl, it's too fresh. If it stands on its end, it's just right. (If it floats, throw it out!)

Cool the eggs in cold water for just a minute to make them cool enough to handle. Try not to refrigerate them before you peel them. Warm eggs seem easier to peel.

It also helps to cook them gently (no vigorous boiling). Start them out with enough cold water to cover them. Some people think it's better to have the eggs at room temperature before they're put on the stove.

Also, some people add salt or vinegar to the cooking water, but we've never seen that make a difference. And some people add a bit of oil. All that seems to do is make them slippery!

Readers add:

• "RE: HB eggs, you didn't mention how long to cook them — my best luck is cover with cold water, bring to boil, reduce heat down for about 10 minutes, turn heat off let stand for about 10 minutes. Roll egg on counter, then peel off shell."

• "I swear by this!! This appliance (Krups 230-70 Egg Express egg cooker) is worth its weight in gold. You will never want to hassle with a pan of boiling water again. The boiled eggs come out perfect. Spend some 'eggstra' money and get one. You won't be sorry."

• "The egg cooker is the only way to go. I have had one for years and never have I had an egg I cannot peel."

Q: **There was a restaurant on 15th Street in the 1960s called Glenn Moore's Tap that served the best shrimp salads. Does anyone have the recipe for it? All I remember was it had shrimp, lettuce, and celery but was great!**

A: Curious Cook columnist Liz Meegan wrote about this dish recently. She was given the recipe by Lucia Moore of Davenport, Glenn Moore's daughter-in-law. Another version was submitted by C.R.G. of Silvis, a former employee of the restaurant.

Lucia Moore told Curious Cook that the entire time her father-in-law was in business, he would not reveal the salad recipe. But then one evening when the family was out for dinner, she asked him for it. Lo and behold, and apparently to her surprise, he gave it to her!

"It turned out to be so easy," Mrs. Moore recalls. "It's funny because so many cookbooks that came out in the

1950s and 1960s all had what they proclaimed was the 'authentic' recipe for the shrimp salad and none were even close."

Glenn Moore's Shrimp Salad

"Use leaf lettuce or Romaine; cut up about ¾ cup celery and add to greens.

"The dressing is: half Kraft (or Hellmann's) Real Mayonnaise and half seafood sauce. I make mine with ½ cup ketchup, 1 full tablespoon horseradish and 1 teaspoon lemon juice," she explains.

"Mix the greens and celery with the shrimp (use fresh, never canned) and then with the dressing.

"Now the guessing is over." — *Lucia Moore*

And here's the way C.R.G. of Silvis remembers Moore's Shrimp Salad:

"I worked as the night cook at Glenn Moore's and my mother was the salad lady who made the Shrimp Salad, which also was popular at night (in the late '50s)," C.R.G. explains. He continues:

"The salad was made of fresh, cut-up shrimp mixed with chopped lettuce. The dressing was very simple: one part mayonnaise and one part cocktail sauce,which was either made by Del Monte or Heinz at the time.

"The above was mixed and put on a large lettuce leaf." — *C.R.G. of Silvis*

Glenn Moore's restaurant was at the corner of 15th Street and 7th Avenue in downtown Moline.

Q: I live in another state. What is the best recipe for making "Maid-Rites"? I'm hungry for a Maid-Rite ... Harris Pizza ... and a bunch of Adolph's Tacos.

A: This questions comes up fairly often, and since we haven't answered it for nearly two years, here goes.

Liz Meegan, who writes the Curious Cook column for The Dispatch/The Rock Island Argus and The Leader, has two "Mock Maid-Rite" recipes on file, as follows:

Mock Maid-Rite No. 1

1 pound ground beef
8 ounces of Coke or Pepsi
Salt and pepper

Brown ground beef, separating as it cooks to form crumbles; drain off fat.

Add salt and pepper to taste. Add Coke or Pepsi and simmer for 20 minutes or until liquid is absorbed. Serve on buns. Makes about 6.

Mock Maid-Rite No. 2

2 pounds lean ground beef (90 percent)
Minced onions, any amount
2 tablespoons Worcestershire sauce
1 can (12 ounces) Coca-Cola or Coke Classic

Brown lean ground beef. Add minced or fresh onion.

Add Worcestershire sauce and can of Coca-Cola after meat is browned. Simmer until liquid evaporates.

For barbecue way: After meat has browned and simmered, add some ketchup, brown sugar and yellow mustard or Boetje's mustard. Let simmer again until nice and warm. (Use a little or a lot of the condiments to make the barbecue sauce.) Serve on buns.

We also found this one, but haven't tried it:

Mock Maid-Rite No. 3

(Darke County (Ohio) Genealogical Society)
1 lb ground beef
1 tsp ground pepper
1 tsp sugar
2 tsp prepared mustard

6 oz beer (optional)
salt (to taste)

Combine ground beef, pepper, sugar, mustard, salt in the top of a double-boiler and add beer. Cover top and heat for one-half hour, stirring occasionally. The longer it cooks, the more the flavors blend together.

Toward the end, uncover to allow some of the liquid to boil off.

Use a slotted serving spoon to serve on hamburger buns with mustard, dill pickles and chopped onion. Serves 6. (Note: Use prepared yellow salad mustard, such as that for hamburgers or hot dogs. Do not use dry powdered mustard, or a Dijoni or Poupon style mustard. Use a good quality, low-fat ground beef. Water may be substituted for beer.)

We also found a Web link for Taylor's Maid-Rite that will allow you to order frozen sandwiches shipped: http://www.maidrite.com/send_maid-rite.html.

There probably are others, as well.

Q: **Are acorns edible for humans?**

A: This time of year, it would be a pretty rotten trick to cheat the squirrels out of them, if you ask us. But if you really want to, you can safely eat an acorn.

People have been doing it for thousands of years. But you don't just crack the shell and eat it raw! Visit http://mail.springer.losaltos.k12.ca.us/1999/19/ohlone/food.html for instructions.

Q: **Does anyone know where I can get the recipe for Subway's**

wonderful white chocolate macadamia nut cookies?

A: It's not possible to get *exactly* the same recipe. For one thing, we learned that Subway gets its cookies from Pillsbury. And the spokeswoman at Pillsbury said the company doesn't give out recipes for products that are made in a large quantity, because the recipe may not scale correctly for a home cook.

So, you have a couple of options. As it happens, Pillsbury does make a ready-to-bake treat that may be close to what you're looking for. It's called Big Deluxe Classics Cookies White Chunk Macadamia Nut.

Or, you could try another recipe for White Chunk Macadamia Nut Cookies.

Here is one from our own Quad-Cities Online Recipe Book, recommended by Liz Meegan, the Curious Cook columnist for The Dispatch and The Rock Island Argus.

It was submitted by Dorothy Wolf of Annawan.

Macadamia Nut Cookies

1 cup butter or margarine, softened
¾ cup white sugar
¾ cup brown sugar
1 teaspoon vanilla extract
2 eggs
2¼ cups flour (all-purpose)
1 teaspoon baking soda
1 teaspoon salt
2 cups white chips
1 cup chopped macadamia nuts

Beat butter or margarine, white and brown sugars and vanilla in mixer until creamy. Beat in eggs, one at a time, beating well. Mix flour, soda and salt together; add to creamed mixture. Stir in white chips and nuts. Drop by tablespoon onto ungreased baking sheets. Preheat oven to 375 degrees. Bake cookies at 375 degrees for 9 to 11 minutes or until browned. Makes 4½ to 5 dozen cookies.

(Good luck, and if you have some extras, our office is at 1810 5th Ave., Moline.)

Q: I once had a recipe for pickled hot peppers that came out as crisp as they were picked from the garden but lost it. Do you know where I might be able to find another one?

A: We consulted food writer Liz Meegan of Moline, who says her copy of The Ball Blue Book Guide to Home Canning, Freezing and Dehydration has a recipe for Hot Pickled Peppers.

We also found a number of similar recipes on the Web (http://www. homecanning.com/usa/ALRecipes. asp?R=76). However, Mrs. Meegan says that food writers only recommend up-to-date canning recipes and directions because older recipes may not be safe by today's standards. She recommends that you get a copy of the book. (It's softcover, and only $4.95.)

Mrs. Meegan writes the Curious Cook column for The Dispatch, The Rock Island Argus and The Leader. If anyone would like to send in a current recipe for Hot Pickled Peppers, we will share it.

Q: Now that it's festival season, what is the difference, if any, between funnel cakes and elephant ears?

A: There's a major difference between Elephant Ears and Funnel Cakes.

Elephant Ears are prepared with a yeast dough. Funnel Cakes are made with a pancake-like batter.

The dough for Elephant Ears may be rolled up like a jelly roll, cut into slices which are pressed into a cinnamon/sugar mixture, sprinkled with nuts, brushed with margarine and more cinnamon/sugar. The rounds are placed on a cookie sheet and baked in the oven.

The yeast dough for Elephant Ears also may be pressed into circles which are fried, one at a time, in hot oil or a deep fryer, drained on paper toweling, brushed with butter, and sprinkled with sugar.

For Funnel Cakes, the pancake-type batter is drizzled into hot oil in a skillet through a funnel in a spiral pattern. *(Thanks for this info to Liz Meegan, writer of our Curious Cook column.)*

Q: Remember the old Dutch Inn in Rock Island, corner of 17th St. and 3rd Ave.? Do you have any info on how to cook their delicious chicken, who did the cooking? Just wish there was a great CHICKEN place like that in the Q-Cs.

A: With great confidence, we sent this question off to the newspaper's Curious Cook, aka Liz Meegan. We figured that if Ms. Meegan didn't know the answer, one of her many readers would. Turns out we were right. Here's what she found out:

Cook's daughter recalls delicious Dutch Inn chicken

It was wonderful to hear from Pamela Langston of Rock Island, who immediately responded to J.F.'s inquiry about who cooked the "delicious chicken" at the old Dutch Inn in Rock Island, "corner of 17th Street and 3rd Avenue."

Mrs. Langston shares with us a bit of history and some good memories:

"My late mother-in-law, Mary Jane Langston, was the cook at The Dutch Inn in the 1930s and early 1940s. I can't remember that she did anything special with the chicken.

"But I remember that she always washed it thoroughly and then dried it on a clean terry towel (no paper towels then!). Then she rolled it in flour and always cooked it in an iron skillet. She used shortening for frying.

"She always said that if she had a nickel for every chicken that she had cut up, she would be a millionaire.

"If you had the chicken and noodles, you had Mary's homemade noodles that she made by working flour into an egg-and-water mixture. Then she rolled it out on cheesecloth and hung it over the backs of the kitchen chairs to dry.

"Mary was a wonderful cook. She made the best bread and cakes and pies and never owned a cookbook.

"I still use her recipe for Potato Salad. No mayonnaise, but a cooked dressing made from a mixture of flour, vinegar, water, eggs and yellow mustard.

"This time of year her kitchen would be like an oven, with no air conditioning and the daylong canning of peaches and tomatoes, which she bought by the bushel basket." — *Pamela Langston*

Readers chime in:

• "I thought that the Dutch Inn downtown Rock Island used what is called a Henny Penny machine or deep fat frier pressure cooker to cook their chicken. I know that the Ship's Wheel that used to be in Andalusia used one, and the chicken was excellent. The Chef's Hat in Bettendorf, which is now closed might also have used one."

• "In regards to the wonderful chicken at the Dutch Inn, I remember it being battered-fried rather than pan-fried. This would have been in the 50's. Also they had a wonderful homemade chicken noodle soup. Does anyone have those recipes?"

• "What about the excellent onion rings they had? That was a meal we ordered as kids."

Q: I love the Coney Island hot dog. They were the best. Does anyone have the recipe for the sauce?

A: The Curious Cook to the rescue again, from a column in February 2003:

D.D. e-mailed a request for a Coney Island recipe. He has fond memories of three local restaurants of yesteryear.

Curious Cook has published similar requests in past columns. We'll try again, but D.D. may have to be content with his memories. D.D. reminisces:

"When I was in high school in 1954, a family owned and operated a 'Coney Island' restaurant on 16th Street, between 5th and 6th avenues, Moline. When you ordered a 'chili dog,' the hot dog was covered with a very smooth chili sauce and if you ordered a bowl of chili the same sauce was served in a bowl.

"It was a very smooth sauce, no chunks of meat or a trace of a bean. It was a very smooth consistency.

"This Coney Island closed but there was in downtown Davenport another Greek family with a 'Coney Island' restaurant and the same chili was served. That restaurant closed when the block was razed for the building of the convention center.

"Then there was one 'Coney Island' left, Harold's Coney Island in Rock Island, just west of the post office. This block also was renovated and now there is no where in the Quad-Cities to get this great taste.

"Curious, can you find this recipe? I long for the taste of the past."

From L.H. of Port Byron, answering the Coney Dog request: "Here is a Texas Sauce (Coney Dog)"

1 can tomato soup
¼ teaspoon dry mustard
1½ pounds ground beef, browned and drained
2 bay leaves
½ teaspoon ground cloves
½ teaspoon paprika
½ teaspoon sugar
1 teaspoon chili powder

Combine all ingredients in large pan. Simmer until thick. (Remove bay leaf before serving.)

Here is another Coney Island Sauce from L.H.:

½ pound ground beef
1 medium onion, diced
1 can (8 ounces) tomato sauce
1 teaspoon chili powder
½ teaspoon Worcestershire sauce

Brown ground beef and onions over medium heat; drain off fat. Add tomato sauce and spices. Bring to boil, reduce heat and simmer 10 minutes.

"Here is a combination, we combined a little out of both," writes L.H.:

Texas Coney Island Sauce
1 pound ground beef
1 can (8 ounces) tomato sauce
1 teaspoon chili powder
½ teaspoon Worcestershire sauce
½ teaspoon paprika
Pinch of ground cloves
1/8 teaspoon dry mustard

Brown ground beef and drain. Add all ingredients. Bring to boil, reduce

heat and simmer for 10 minutes. — *L.H. Port Byron*

(And here is more published in September 2002:)

Coney Island Sauce

V.M. of Rock Island sent this recipe for Coney Island Sauce for S.N. of Milan. V.M. says she clipped the recipe from a Curious Cook column about 10 years ago.

½ pound ground beef
3 tablespoons vinegar
2 tablespoons Worcestershire sauce
1 tablespoon sugar
1 teaspoon chili powder
1 teaspoon paprika
¼ teaspoon black pepper
¼ teaspoon cayenne pepper (red pepper)
½ teaspoon salt
¾ cup ketchup
¼ cup barbecue sauce
1 cup water

Brown the ground beef and drain off excess fat. Add all other ingredients, mixing well. Simmer until thick, about 1 hour.

Note: For a thicker sauce, you can use 1 pound of ground beef. — *V.M. of Rock Island*

A reader adds: "The Coney Island restaurant was on 16th Street between 5th and 6th Avenues, in downtown Moline, and was owned and operated by the Dellos family. The health department, nowadays, probably would have a fit over their practice of displaying their savory food items, unrefrigerated, in the front window of the restaurant. I graduated, from the "old" Moline High School, with one of the daughters, Angeline, in 1951 and spent many a memorable after-school experience at the Coney Island sampling their "gourmet" Coney Dogs, which I think sold for the enormous sum of 15 cents each."

The Quad-Cities & Quad-Citians

Q: My friend and I have been arguing about exactly which cities are the Quad-Cities — which ones are?

A: Depends on who you ask. Earlier this century, the region was referred to as the Tri-City area, and everybody could agree on Davenport, Rock Island and Moline.

The term Quad-Cities was coined at least as early as the 1920s to include the fourth-largest city, East Moline; but in the 1960s and '70s, burgeoning Bettendorf shot past East Moline in population and staked its own claim as the fourth "Quad-City." Some started using the name Quint-Cities to avoid the controversy, but "Quad" seems to have stuck.

Q: We use Weyerhauser copy paper at work, and knowing there is a Weyerhaeuser family plot at Chippiannock Cemetery in Rock Island, is this the lumber baron from Rock Island's plot and is he related to the company that makes copy paper?

A: Yes, and yes.

Lumber baron Frederick Weyerhaeuser began his career in a lumber yard in Coal Valley. At one time he was considered the richest man in the world.

He was born on Nov. 21, 1834 in Germany. His father, a vintner, died when Mr. Weyerhaeuser was 12 years old. Mr. Weyerhaeuser came to Rock Island in 1856.

He went to work on the construction of the Rock Island and Peoria Railway, later a part of the Rock Island Railroad. "Soon after," according to The Daily Dispatch, in a 1914 article, "he took a position as night fireman at the sawmill operated by Mead, Smith and Marsh in Rock Island." Mr. Weyerhaeuser eventually became the supervisor of the mill.

In 1857 Mead, Smith and Marsh opened a lumber yard in Coal Valley and put Mr. Weyerhaeuser in charge. That same year Mr. Weyerhaeuser married Sara Elizabeth Bloedel. She had come from Erie, Pa., to visit her sister, Mrs. F.C.A. Denkmann. Both Mr. and Mrs. Weyerhaeuser had come from the same village in Germany.

Mr. Weyerhaeuser eventually bought the lumber business in Coal Valley and formed a partnership with his brother-in-law F.C.A. Denkmann. They acquired a bankrupt sawmill in Rock Island after there was a fire near the mill.

Eventually other sawmills in Rock Island, Davenport and Milan were merged with Weyerhaeuser & Denkmann. Logs were cut for the mills along the Chippewa and St. Croix rivers in northern Wisconsin and driven down these rivers.

Then the logs were made into rafts to come down the Mississippi River to Rock Island.

The local mills of Weyerhaeuser and Denkmann covered 30 acres. The plants turned about 40 million feet of pine lumber annually with lath and shingles.

(Interesting note: Because he was familiar with the strict forestry conservation practices in Europe, Mr. Weyerhaeuser recognized that this country would lose its forests in time. He rounded up the leading timber owners in the country and took them to Washington to see President Theodore Roosevelt. The meeting

influenced the president's campaign for the conservation of natural resources, which is still reflected in federal policy today.)

As Midwestern timber supplies diminished, Mr. Weyerhaeuser looked to forests in the West. He moved to Minnesota in 1891. In January 1900, he and 15 partners formed the Weyerhaeuser Timber Co. in the Northwest, the date of its corporate birthday.

He died suddenly on April 4. 1914. And he is buried in Chippiannock Cemetery in Rock Island.

The Denkmann family remained in Rock Island. Mr. Denkmann died at age 81 in early 1905. The Rock Island mills closed six months later.

There are many reminders of the Weyerhaeuser family still here. The Rock Island Library, at 4th Avenue and 19th Street, opened in 1903 and cost $85,000.

The library was made possible by a $50,000 loan by Weyerhauser and donations from him and Denkmann.

Augustana's House on the Hill was the home of the Weyerhaeuser family before being given to the college.

Hauberg Civic Center, 1300 24th St., Rock Island, was the home of Susanne C. Denkmann (1872 -1942), Mr. Denkmann's youngest daughter.

Q: Why hasn't the Quad-Cities consolidated into one city under one mayor, police force, fire department, etc? It seems that funds and taxes could better be distributed for large projects and expenses if the Quad-Cities did consolidate, at least on the Illinois side of the river.

A: Several serious attempts at consolidating municipalities on the Illinois side have been made over the years, but the idea has never appealed greatly to most residents.

The most recent try at consolidation came on March 21, 2000, when voters in Moline and East Moline overwhelming rejected a proposal to join the two cities. The vote was 8,306 to 3,221 against the merger. Eighty-three percent of voters in East Moline opposed the idea, as did 64 percent of those in Moline.

In 1988, voters in Moline, Rock Island, East Moline, Hampton and Coal Valley were asked to create "Super City" — a single municipality of about 115,000 people. The proposal was defeated by a ratio of nearly 2-1 despite widespread backing from civic leaders and various community groups.

In 1965, the idea also was discussed but never made it to the ballot.

Forty years before that, in 1925, residents in Moline and East Moline voted on a proposed merger. Though the overall vote was 2,906 to 2,155 in favor, the idea died since it had to be aproved by a majority in both cities and East Moliners overwhelming said "no."

The consolidation idea lives on, though, with the creation of a "Quad-Cities Interstate Metropolitan Authority" being the current focus. The so-called Metro Authority would cover both Scott County, Iowa, and Rock Island County, Illinois, and would be responsible primarily for transportation issues, such as a new Mississippi River bridge. Various studies are under way, though no vote has been called in either county.

Q: Who is the most famous person from the Quad-Cities?

A: Good question. We assembled a panel of "experts" from The Dispatch and the Rock Island Argus to help on this one.

First off, just like editors, they wanted to define what you meant by "from" the Quad-Cities. Does that mean the person had to be born here, or nearby, or just had to live here for awhile?

We also noticed that "famous" depends on your outlook. Sports fans figured we'd all know Roger Craig. Music fans were shocked that not everyone had heard of Louie Bellson. And age matters: You'll only know June Haver if you like old movies.

The most-often-named were John Deere and Bix Beiderbecke, but we'll list all our top picks here and we'll let *you* make the final choice. They're in alphabetical order.

- *Eddie Albert* — Born Edward Albert Heimberger, this Rock Island native became the star of the TV series, "Green Acres."

- *Bix Beiderbecke* — jazz cornetist who played hard in the Roaring '20s and died at the age of 28 in 1931

Bix Beiderbecke

- *Louie Bellson* — jazz drummer who has played with many of the world's top musicians; husband of the late Pearl Bailey.

- *Ken Berry* — actor and dancer best known for roles in TV's "F-Troop" and "Mayberry R.F.D."; attended Moline junior high and high schools.

- *Black Hawk* — war leader of the Sauk and Mesquakie (Fox) nations, he lived in the Indian village of Saukenuk in what is now Rock Island.

Black Hawk

- *Isabel Bloom* — artist most noted for unique concrete sculptures; died in 2001, but her name and sculptures live on in products produced by Isabel Bloom L.L.C., headquartered in Moline.

- *John Bloom* — met his wife Isabel while studying under artist Grant Wood in Stone City, Iowa, in the 1930s; known as a "New Deal" artist. You may have seen his bronze sculpture of two boys called "Waiting for the Ferry" on Davenport's riverfront.

- *Suzy Bogguss* — multi-platinum-selling country singer from Aledo.

- *Max Allan Collins* — mystery novelist, movie producer, director, screenwriter, comic-book author and musician, the Muscatine resident wrote the graphic novel on which the Tom Hanks' movie "Road to Perdition" was based.

Suzy Bogguss

- *Buffalo Bill Cody* — American scout and showman was born in Scott County, near Princeton; his "Wild West" shows toured Europe and the U.S. from 1883 to 1916; his family's homestead is now the Cody Museum.

- *Roger Craig* — National Football League all-pro running back, helped lead the San Francisco 49ers to three

Super Bowl titles; an all-state athlete at Davenport Central High School.

John Deere

• *John Deere* — developed the revolutionary self-scouring steel plow in 1837, and moved to Moline to found Deere & Co.

• *June Haver* — born in Rock Island, starred in many films of the '40s and '50s.

• *D.D. Palmer* — formulated the theories which spurred modern chiropractic medicine and founded Palmer School of Chiropractic in Davenport, the world's oldest chiropractic institution.

• *Ronald Reagan* — former U.S. president and actor began his career as a radio announcer at Davenport's WOC in 1931; born in Tampico, Ill., about 40 miles east of the Quad-Cities.

Ronald Reagan

• *Marjabelle Stewart* — Kewanee, Ill., resident is a leading national columnist and teacher on etiquette.

• *Tennessee Gov. Don Sundquist* — former resident of Moline and graduate of Augustana College.

A reader adds: "You left out Jude Cole, who was either from Carbon Cliff or East Moline, not sure which."

Singer/songwrite Jude Cole is a native of East Moline. His top 10 hits include "Baby It's Tonight." He did make the top Quad-Cities entertainers of the 20th century, as chosen by The Dispatch and The Rock Island Argus in 2000: 1. Bix Beiderbecke; 2. Louis Bellson; 3. Susan Glaspell; 4. Buffalo Bill Cody; 5. Margherita Roberti; 6. Harry R. "Tim" Moore; 7. Charlie Correll; 8. June Haver; 9. Mary Beth Peil; 10. Ken Barry; 11. Alice French; 12. Mary Fluhrer Nighswander; 13. Don Wooten; 14. Paul Norton; 15. Max Allan Collins; 16. Susann McDonald; 17. Mary Lou Dennhardt; 18. Suzy Bogguss; 19. Father E.M. Catich; 20. Isabel Bloom; 21. David Collins; 22. Stuart Margolin; 23. Maurine Englin; 24. Bill Bell; 25. Jude Cole; 26. Murray Hickey Ley; 27. Jesse Johnson; 28. G. LaVerne Flambo; 29. Darrell Bush; 30. (tie) Billy Peiffer and Laurdine "Pat" Patrick.

Another reader says: "For your famous QC people list you could add Lara Flynn Boyle, who was born in Davenport."

Thanks for the heads-up. The actress was born March 24, 1970, in Davenport, but moved to Chicago at age 6 and grew up there. Most would know her as assistant district attorney Helen Gamble on television's "The Practice."

Other readers add:

• "Who is the most famous person … ? If it wasn't for Col. George Davenport, there probably wouldn't be a lot of these other 'famous' people. He and his three children have contributed greatly to the development of this area."

Col. George Davenport

69

• "You should also include Farmer Miller, an old-time boxer from the '20s and '30s who won a number of Golden Gloves before going pro. He is still talked about today from some of the older fighters."

• "You left out Bonnie Bartlett of 'St. Elsewhere' fame on your most famous list."

• "For a sports figure, I think more famous than Roger Craig is Rock Island native Don Nelson, for years one of the best coaches in the NBA."

• "I would rank John Bald as another famous artist from the Quad-Cities."

• "I think you forgot Don Nelson, native of R.I., in your famous people from the Q-C's. He played in the NBA but is more famous as a longtime coach in the NBA and currently coaches the Dallas Mavericks. Thanks. It is still a great list you came up with."

• "Hey guys, isn't Dallas Mavericks head coach and former All-American college basketball player from the University of Iowa Don Nelson a Rock Island native? He should be on the 'most famous' Quad-Citians list."

• "For your roster of famous persons, how about Spike O'Dell, WGN, Chicago morning personality?"

• "These are some people you left out on famous people from the Quad-Cities, I know that on the show "St. Elsewhere" there was a female actress on there that played one of the doctors, she was the thin gray shoulder lengthed haired doctor, that grew up in Moline, IL, I know someone that is good friends with her that could give her name. Also we forgot Charlie Brown who boxed … Michael Nunn another famous boxer, also dethroened.

"We have Adam Lingner who went to Alleman High School that went on to the NFL as well as Ron Hallstrom who went to Moline High School that

either went famous for basketball or football, I can't remember. Then there's the actor John Getz who grew up on 13th street right across the street from my grandmother's house, he did a sitcom with Cybill Shepherd … he has also starred in many sitcoms and major motion pictures. There is also Roger Craig from Davenport Iowa that went to the NFL as well. I am sure if we go further into it, we will find out many other people that made it big that were from the Quad-Cities, ccc'mon people, lets put our thinking caps on … Hope these help!"

• "Sue Lyon — 'Lolita' from Davenport. I was a 12-year-old resident of Rock Island when the movie 'Lolita' was showing at the Fort in Rock Island or at either the Capitol or RKO in Davenport … I don't remember which. I remember all the old folks in the Quad-Cities gossiping about the film at that time."

You're right. Sue Lyon was born July 10, 1946, in Davenport. Film critic Leonard Maltin says:

"She was only 13 and a total 'unknown' when cast as the angelfaced nymphet who was the underaged object of James Mason's affections in Stanley Kubrick's controversial 'Lolita' (1962), but her performance raised moviegoers' pulses and, to coin a phrase, a star was born."

Q: Someone told me a woman from Davenport named Glaspell once won a Pulitzer Prize. Is that true?

A: Yes, it is.

Susan Glaspell, born in Davenport in 1876, in 1931 became the second woman ever to receive a Pulitzer, for her play *Alison's House*. In all, she produced fifty short stories, fourteen plays, and nine novels before her death in 1948 in Provincetown, Mass.

She and her husband, George Cram Cook, also a Davenporter, founded the Provincetown Players, a theater group that eventually grew to include such luminaries as Eugene O'Neill and Edna St. Vincent Millay.

There's a quick summary of Ms. Glaspell's life on this Web site: http://www.unlv.edu/faculty/droisen/glaspell.htm.

Q: How can the Quad City "International" Airport call itself an INTERNATIONAL airport when there are no international flights either leaving or departing?

A: The choice in a name is up to the airport board, and on March 19, 1997, it decided to add "international" to the airport's name.

The rationale board members acted upon was outlined in this news story about the change:

Q-C Airport goes international
MOLINE — With a single, unanimous vote Tuesday, airport commissioners changed the name of the Quad City Airport to the Quad City International Airport.

The change reflects the Quad-Cities' U.S. Customs port-of-entry status obtained in 1986, airport director of aviation Kent George said.

It also reflects the start of direct air-cargo services to Mexico earlier this month.

Travelers will not see any change in existing air services because of the name change, Mr. George said.

"It's a recognition that we have been an international airport for several years," Mr. George said. "We're the only other airport in Iowa and Illinois, outside of Chicago, that has direct delivery of international cargo. A lot of airports call themselves 'international,' but don't use the services. We have had the services, but didn't have the name."

The name change may mean the most to Quad-Cities' cheerleader John Gardner, who, as president of the Quad City Development Group, markets the community to out-of-town companies. Mr. Gardner suggested the name change in a letter to the airport authority more than a year ago.

Mr. Gardner said Tuesday he was "thrilled" with the airport's official new name. The designation was "a very important step," he said. "It confirms what we are trying to tell companies, especially to global companies we're trying to locate here, that they can make international connections from the Quad City Airport."

That type of information is more vital to companies outside the Midwest and less familiar with the community, he said. The international designation is a factor the communities of Des Moines and Cedar Rapids in Iowa and others in Illinois have used effectively, Mr. Gardner said. Now, the Quad-Cities has the same advantage, he said. — *By Rita Pearson, staff writer*

Q: What type of political entity is the Metropolitan Airport Authority and to whom is it responsible?

A: The MAA is a special taxing district created under the auspices of the Illinois Airport Authority Act, which was passed by the Legislature

71

and went into effect April 5, 1945. The act provided that local airport authorities possessing taxing and bonding powers could be created by referendum.

On Nov. 10, 1947, voters in seven Rock Island County townships — Moline, South Moline, Rock Island, South Rock Island, Black Hawk, Coal Valley and Hampton — voted by a 2-1 ratio to create the Metropolitan Airport Authority.

The authority originally had six members, but that number has increased to seven. The chairman of the Rock Island County Board appoints two, and the mayors of Rock Island, Moline, East Moline, Milan and Silvis each appoint one. The commissioners, as they are called, are therefore responsible to the county board chairman and mayors, and through them to the residents of the seven townships.

Illinois' Airport Authority Act was inspired, at least in part, by competition between Moline and Davenport to be the site of THE Quad-Cities' airport.

The federal Civil Aeronautics Administration (now the Federal Aviation Administration) created a furor in the Illinois Quad-Cities in the early 1940s by earmarking funds to create a major airport for the area at Mount Joy, north of Davenport. Illinois-side interests were outraged and argued with considerable justification that the Moline airport was already a major hub, while the one in Mount Joy was little more than a landing strip.

Illinois Gov. Dwight Green promised to aid the Illinois side in the fight, and the Airport Authority Act was one result. The CAA eventually reversed its decision to back the Mount Joy airport.

The Moline airport, originally known as Franing Field and privately operated, was as early as 1910 (just seven years after the Wright Brothers' first flight) designated by the U. S. Army as a control point for coast-to-coast air journeys. In 1926, airmail service was added and, in 1927, regular passenger and freight service was available.

Moline assumed ownership of the field in 1935 and held it until the Metropolitan Airport Authority took over after the 1947 referendum.

While most of the airport's $22 million-plus annual budget is covered by money from the federal government and from various fees, the MAA collects about $1 million per year in property taxes from residents of the seven townships that created the authority in 1947. The occasional suggestion that the local tax base should be broadened to include the entire bi-state region served by the airport runs into stiff opposition, particularly in Iowa.

Memories are long, and the disputes of the 1940s live on even though the main players in them are long dead.

Q: Who was the baseball player from East Moline who won an all-star game in the 1960s?

A: Dean Stone attended United Township High School in East Moline but actually lived in Silvis. His all-star win came in 1954.

The win was unusual — Stone did not get a single batter out. Playing for the American League, he entered the game with the AL trailing 9-8 with two outs in the eighth inning. Red Schoendienst, on third, tried to steal home but Stone's throw nailed him for the third out. The AL rallied in the 9th inning to win.

Incidentally, 1954 was both Stone's rookie year and the best of his career.

He was 12-10 with a lackluster Washington Senators team that won only 66 games. He bounced around with a half-dozen teams over the next eight years, finishing with a 29-39 lifetime record.

Q: I remember a while back we had twin brothers go to the Olympics. Where were they from and what were their names?

A: Darrin and Dan Steele were from Sherrard. After missing an expected trip to the 1996 Summer Olympics in track events when both were injured in trials, they switched focus and went to both the 1998 and 2002 games as bobsledders.

Dan got a bronze medal as part of the U. S. four-man bobsled team in 2002. Darrin finished ninth in the two-man event.

A reader adds: "As I recall, an autographed helmet from the Steele brothers lives in a display case in the commons area of Sherrard High School."

Q: I am currently aboard the USS Nimitz, deployed on our 7th month of cruise. I am from the Quad-Cities getting ready to return soon. Okay, here is the question ... I'm reading the book "Ghost Soldiers" by Hampton Sides about the Cabanatuan prison camp in the Philippines. He writes of an American guerrilla named Robert Lapham, said to be from Davenport. I have searched and searched and cannot find any records of a Mr.

Lapham being from the Q-C; the only being from Michigan. Do you know of any records of a Mr. Lapham from the Q-C?

A: Yes, indeed, the Robert Lapham mentioned in "Ghost Soldiers" was a native of Davenport.

He was serving in the Philippines when World War II began. When American forces there surrendered in early 1942, he faded into the jungle and waged guerrilla warfare against the Japanese until the war's end.

When "Ghost Soldiers" was published in 2001, Mr. Lapham's hometown newspaper, the Quad City Times, did a feature recalling his adventures.

Among other things, the story said that when Mr. Lapham returned to Davenport after the war, 25,000 people turned out for a welcome-home parade.

Mr. Lapham co-authored his own book, "Lapham's Raiders: Guerrillas in the Philippines 1942-1945," published in 1996. It's available at http://www.amazon.com.

At the time of the 2001 feature story, Mr. Lapham, 84, was living in Sun City, Ariz.

Q: Was Black Hawk really a chief or was he a war leader?

A: Two things can be said with certainty:

1. Black Hawk was a war leader, a man of great skill and courage whom Sauk warriors willingly followed into battle for 40 years or more.

2. He was not THE chief, in the sense that he commanded the Sauks in all civil, religious and military affairs.

Whether he was *A* chief is, it seems to us, little more than a matter of semantics. What *is* the difference between "war leader" and "war chief"?

Black Hawk is referred to as "Chief" or "War Chief" in countless works, including many contemporaneous with his lifetime. That, however, may reflect an ignorance of Sauk culture and tradition among the writers and perhaps should not be given much weight.

On the other hand, the Illinois State Preservation Agency, in its Web page for Black Hawk State Historic Site (http://www.state.il.us/hpa/Blackhawk.htm), refers to "The Sauk warrior Black Hawk (he was not a chief) …"

The official position of The Dispatch/Argus (Quad-Cities Online's parent organization) is that Black Hawk was a war leader, not a chief, though each new reporter seems sooner or later to call him a chief and thereby stirs up a letter writer or two who feels strongly on the subject.

Worth noting, too, is that Black Hawk never referrred to himself as a chief in his "Autobiography of Ma-Ka-Tai-Me-She-Kia-Kiak, or Black Hawk."

He talks instead of finding warriors willing to follow him, even when he was a teenager, as a result of his actions in battle.

The complete autobiography can be found on Northern Illinois University's library Web site (http://lincoln.lib.niu.edu/cgi-bin/navigate?/lib35/artfl1/databases/sources/IMAGE/.2200). Included there is an affidavit from Antoine LeClaire, to whom Black Hawk dictated the autobiography, attesting that the work accurately reflects what the fabled warrior told him.

Q: During WWII, a Moline man placed several Bazookas under the wings of His Piper Cub Scout plane. He then used the plane to attack German tanks. I believe his name was Carpentier or Carpenter. Can you give me any more information?

A: Charles "Bazooka Charlie" Carpenter, a native of Edgington in southern Rock Island County, graduated from Rock Island High School and Centre College in Danville, Ky. He was teaching history at Moline High School when he joined the Army in 1942.

In 1944, by then a major, he arrived in France, where his assignment was flying a Piper Cub on reconnaissance

Major Charles Carpenter with his plane, "Rosie the Rocketeer," somewhere in France. His battlefield exploits in the tiny plane won him a variety of nicknames: "Bazooka Charlie," "The Mad Major" and "Lucky Carpenter." (File Photo)

missions in front of the 4th Armoured Division of Gen. George Patton's Third Army. Ignoring regulations against arming the tiny recon planes, Major Carpenter attached six bazooka launchers to the wings of "Rosie the Rocketeer" and began attacking German armor. Threatened with court-martial, he was spared that fate by Gen. Patton himself, who not only stopped the disciplinary proceedings but awarded the major a medal for bravery.

Major Carpenter was soon known the world over. The Army newspaper, Stars and Stripes, featured him and his exploits several times, as did papers as far-flung as the New York Sun and the London Times. The Associated Press reporter Wes Gallagher, in a 1945 article in Liberty Magazine, said Major Carpenter was "a legend in an outfit where reckless bravery is commonplace."

He told Gallagher that his idea of fighting a war was "to attack, attack and then attack again." By war's end, Major Carpenter had destroyed six German tanks, participated in several ground fights (he'd land on the battlefield and lend a hand), won a Silver Star and an Air Medal and been promoted to lieutenant colonel.

Discharged from the Army after it was discovered he had Hodgkins disease, he was given just two years to live. He made it for 20 years; he died in 1966 in Urbana, where he had taught school since the war's end. He is buried at Edgington Cemetery.

Q: Where could I find a list of the Quad City Men that were killed in the Viet Nam undeclared war?

A: Following is a list compiled by The Vietnam Veterans of America, Quad-Cities chapter. It contains 86 names, 48 Rock Island County soldiers and 38 from Scott County. Ed Gaudet of Davenport, a trustee of the group, said he believes it is complete.

Rock Island County

Ricky J. Almanza, Moline; Terry L. Banning, Andalusia; Carl T. Bauer, Rock Island; James J. Bishop, Moline; William W. Boetje, Moline; James J. Branham, Moline; Dennis W. Brown, Moline; Jerry L. Danay, Rock Island; Donald L. Dryoel, Rock Island; Danny W. Engesser, Rock Island; Mark A. Foster, Rock Island; John B. Golz, Rock Island; Darwin D. Gordon, Rock Island; George R. Graham, Port Byron. Allen E. Guy, Rock Island; Roger E. Jarvis, Moline; Michael A. Johnson, Moline; Michael R. Kale, Moline; Timothy W. Kearney, Rock Island; James M. King, Rock Island; Kenneth J. Knoeferl, Rock Island; Thomas L. Larson, Rock Island; Wayne M. Lenderman, Rock Island; Donald G. Lukens, Moline; Paul L. Marchant, Moline; Joseph V. Mathias, Moline; Stephen C. Moseley, Moline. Randall A. Olson, Moline; David W. Ranson, Rock Island; James D. Raychel, East Moline; George P. Reed, Milan; William J. Risse, Moline; Charles J. Rogiers, Rock Island; Leroy A. Rost, Moline; Leroy F. Schyska, Moline; Arthur D. Sinksen, Rock Island; John C. Smith, Moline; Rolleen C. Sorim, Moline; Raymond R. Varner Jr., Moline; Paul P. Vavrosky, Milan; Gale K. Vogler, East Moline; David B. Wainwright, Port Byron; Michael J. Warren, Moline; Robert L. Webster, Moline; Barry S. Wells, Moline; Michael K. Wonderlich, Moline; James P. Woner, East Moline; James L. Wood, Rock Island.

Scott County

Wayne R. Anderson, Bettendorf; Michael R. Ball, Davenport; Alan R.

Boone, Davenport; Philip D. Cheek, Davenport; Jerry P. Clark, Davenport; James B. Cook, Bettendorf; Lowell L. Crawford, Davenport; Jerry W. Cutting, Davenport; David K. Ditch; Davenport. William D. Farrel, Davenport; Donald L. Fleetword, Davenport; Carl R. Foster, Davenport; Patrick L. Fricke, LeClaire; Larry M. Gronewold, Donahue; Michael D. Hahn, Davenport; Wayne G. Hubbard, Davenport; David W. Jones, Davenport; Edward W. Knapper, Eldridge; James B. Laird, Davenport; William E. Leamon, Davenport; Joseph A. Maag, LeClaire; Michael K.

Maloney, Davenport; Charles A. Morse, Davenport. Gary A. Neavor, Bettendorf; Carl J. Olson, Davenport; Jesse J. Pena, Davenport; Frank J. Quinland Jr., Davenport; Gary K. Rath, Davenport; George P. Rogers, Bettendorf; Joseph A. Schwerdtfeger, Davenport; Norbert G. Simmons, Davenport; Reid W. Stoltenberg, Bettendorf; John E. Swanson Jr., Davenport; Michael J. Utter, Davenport; Robert J. Voss, Davenport; David H. Wilkerson, Davenport; John J. Wilson, Davenport; Daniel L. Wisely, Davenport.

Odds & Ends

Q: When you see a sign on the highway that states the mileage to the next town, where in the next town does the distance refer to? I always heard it was the post office.

A: We, too, have heard that the post office was the reference point. But that may or may not be the case.

John Wegmeyer of the Illinois Department of Transportation said the distance is measured to the "center of the city."

The Iowa Department of Transportation, in the FAQ section of its Web site, explains it this way: "The mileage shown on distance signs is the distance to a point near the center of the community. A public building such as a post office, city hall or courthouse is used as a point of reference for the center of the community. The mileage is rounded to the nearest mile."

Q: Is there really a "Patriotic Rock" in rural Iowa?

A: Yes, there is. It's southwest of Des Moines, near the town of Greenfield.

The Greenfield Web site (http://www.greenfieldiowa.com/patriotic_rock.htm) has an information page and pictures.

Q: What is the history of Cry Baby Bridge (off of 230th Street outside of Viola, Ill.) Rumor has it that it was the scene of a crash where children were killed and is now haunted by their ghosts.

There are directions to this bridge on 2dorks.com … It states that if you put your car in neutral that you will be pushed across the bridge.

A: We couldn't find anything in our files about this specific Cry Baby Bridge, but we did discover there are lots of bridges by the same name all over the country. You'll also find haunted Cry Baby Hill here and there, or Cry Baby Lane. It seems to be a popular ghost story theme.

If you're looking for spooky tales close to home, here are some we compiled last year:

• *Palmer College of Chiropractic's Pi Kappa Chi fraternity house at 731 Main St.* Students and administrators have heard and seen odd things, felt they were being watched, and even choked! The fraternity brought in Chicago psychic Irene Hughes in 1972, and she identified the ghost as a long-dead medical doctor who had lived in the house. A check of the abstract verified that information.

• *A home in Davenport's McClellan Heights neighborhood, which was part of the Old Camp McClellan, a Civil War mustering point.* The home had a room filled with a cold wind where children would wake up crying in the night. A Mrs. Hughes was called to that home, too, and said she saw a man dressed in blue whom nobody else could see — a soldier. She also saw a stockade and Indians being mistreated, and that squared with history. Indians were imprisoned in a stockade in Davenport after an uprising in Minnesota during the Civil War.

• *Another big, old house on Ripley Street in Davenport occupied by students.* It said to have a haunted attic, which scared pets in the home, and a transparent "gray-brown figure that appeared to be a man" in the living room. When one of the roomers started to make a lot of changes in the house, the ghosts bugged him so much that he moved out.

- *Two popular tales deal with ghosts related to Augustana College's bell tower and its Andreen Hall.* Legend has it that Andreen Hall is haunted by the ghost of a former student who took his own life many years ago.

- *A popular ghost story is about the black angel.* The black angel was a statue of at the Deere tomb in Riverside Cemetery in Moline. According to legend, the stone statue turned black as it stood its quiet vigil over the cemetery.

Local young people used the statue as a test of bravery. The idea was to run through the cemetery at the stroke of midnight and touch the angel.

Many stories were told of the luckless people who did not escape the angel, a young man who touched the angel and died of a heart attack, and a young woman who spent the night in the cemetery, and then was found unconscious and with her hair turned white. The statue eventually had to be removed to prevent vandalism at the cemetery.

- *Another legend is "the house that isn't there," just outside the Quad-Cities.* (The property owner asked that the location not be revealed.)

According to legend, the house appears in a pasture where the real house once existed. A clump of trees silhouetted against the sky slowly merges into the shape of a house complete with windows and shapes moving behind them. Sometimes shapes are seen moving in the meadow in front of the house. One story says there was a house of freed slaves on the plot during the late 1800s which was destroyed with the occupants inside.

- *Some say the ghost of slain restaurateur Nick Chirekos walks the old Velie mansion in Moline, from its days as the popular Plantation restaurant and night club.* Mr. Chirekos, 59, was shot to death in 1979 on the second floor of the sprawling Velie villa nearby. He unknowingly walked in as a man was robbing his office safe. One tale has several kitchen employees hearing Nick's voice.

A former bartender said he entered The Plantation's locked Tahitian Room a couple months after the murder and "heard a man clear his throat." Family and friends say it's all nonsense.

Q: Are there any places in the Quad-Cities that are documented to be haunted?

A: Documented? How about "rumored" to be haunted instead?

For more info, go to the library and check out books by Bruce Carlson, a writer in Fort Madison, Iowa, entitled "Ghosts of Rock Island County, Illinois" and "Ghosts of Scott County, Iowa."

Q: I am trying to restore my father's 1927 Buddy L dump truck. Is there a museum in the area, where I may view artifacts, history, pictures, etc? Does anyone know of a business or individual in town that

specializes in toy restoration or steel fabrication?

A: There have been special exhibits of Buddy L toys in the Quad-Cities several times over the years, but the only permanent one we know of is a part of the Putnam Museum's "River, Prairie and People" collection.

As you know, Buddy L Toys were first built in 1921 by The Moline Pressed Steel Co. The line was soon purchased by The Bettendorf Co., which manufactured Buddy L toys for a number of years. Ownership of the name has since changed several times, and is currently held by Imperial Toy Co., headquartered in Los Angeles.

Imperial's Web site (http://www.imperialtoy.com/buddyl_about.asp) has a brief history of Buddy L and a gallery of old Buddy L toys.

We don't know offhand of anyone specializing in toy restoration. Perhaps one of our readers will be able to help.

A reader advises that you might want to contact Ron Aust of Davenport, a well-known toy expert and collector. Mr. Aust frequently organizes local shows for toys and collectibles.

Q: In America, if all east-west highways end in even numbers, and all north-south highways end in odd numbers; can you please explain I-74?

A: It's all a matter of perspective. In the Quad-Cities, and western Illlinois for that matter, I-74 certainly runs north-south.

But over its entire course it is an east-west road. Its western terminus is in Davenport, at its junction with I-80; its eastern terminus is in Cincinnati, Ohio, which is more east than south of the Quad-Cities.

To be slightly more precise: The western terminus of I-74 is at latitude 41° 35' North and longitude 90° 31' West; the eastern terminus is at latitude 39° 08' North and longitude 84° 32' West.

Each degree of latitude (north-south measurement) represents approximately 69 miles, so I-74 runs about 170 miles north and south. The distance represented by each degree of longitude (east-west measurement) varies from about 69 miles at the equator to nothing at the poles; in the latitudes through which I-74 runs, each degree represents roughly 50 miles, so I-74 runs about 300 miles east and west.

Long-range plans for I-74 envision it being extended into South Carolina at some far-distant date. Even if that comes to pass, it will still be more an east-west than a north-south road.

Q: On many businesses (such as the paint factory in Port Byron) is a sign stating ISO 9001. What does this mean?

A: ISO stands for International Standards Organization.

ISO 9001 is an internationally accepted manufacturing standard developed in Geneva, Switzerland, in 1987 by the International Standards Organization. It establishes quality control management systems for processes ranging from structural design and manufacturing to service and distribution of the finished product.

ISO 9001 is recognized by 80 countries, including the United States. So U.S. manufacturers strive for the ISO certification to sell products on a global basis.

It's a good thing, and that's why the companies that have earned it generally have a big party, and paint ISO on their signs. But they can't rest — the ISO certificate has to be renewed periodically.

Q: Recently I was at the Botanical Center and noticed a group of ladies with red hats touring and receiving a lesson on plants. Is there a red hat group in the QCA? What is their purpose and how can you join?

A: You were seeing members of the Crimson Chapeaux of the Quad City Botanical Center, one of the local chapters of the Red Hat Society.

The statement of purpose on their Web site explains what it's all about: "The Red Hat Society began as a result of a few women deciding to greet middle age with verve, humor, and elan. We believe silliness is the comedy relief of life, and, since we are all in it together, we might as well join red-gloved hands and go for the gusto together. Underneath the frivolity, we share a bond of affection, forged by common life experiences and a genuine enthusiasm for wherever life takes us next."

It seems to be a pretty fun group with few rules. You don't have to be a certain age to join, but you can't wear a Red Hat until you're 50. Men are not eligible even if they are willing to wear a red hat, as we understand it.

Tea parties seem to be the main event.

Q: I have viewed many barges up and down the river. As the barges are tied together there is a pipe-type device on the very first barge that is lowered into the water. Do you know if it is a steering device? Or some kind of lighting rod device?

A: No, we didn't know that that pipe-type device is, though we've also noticed it on passing barges. So we turned to the U. S. Army Corps of Engineers for help.

The answer from the Corps public affairs office: "It is a transducer for the bow-mounted depth finder. Depth finders are mounted on the front of the barge and on the back in the tow. Sometimes, one transducer will be mounted on each corner at the front of the barges. The depth finder prevents them from running aground."

Q: I'm curious as to why and when Silvis stopped hosting the Silvis Country Music Festival. As a child growing up a few blocks away from the location of the annual festivities I used to look forward to the crowds, music, drunken debauchery, and the thrill of seeing if I could jump the fences without being caught. Where did it go?

A: The Silvis Country Music Festival ended its 21-year-run after the 1995 event. The organizers — the Silvis Fire Department, Silvis Optimist Club and East Moline-Silvis Kiwanis Club — decided to give it up after making only $175.41 that year after paying expenses of $93,885.81. The year's meager return continued a trend that was several years long.

That's not much of a return for the endless hours it took members of the organizations to plan and stage each year's two-day event, which at its peak drew as many as 20,000 people per night and was said to be the largest country music festival in Illinois.

Ironically enough, the festival's demise was caused in great part by country music's increasing popularity. All around the country, more venues (including The Mark of the Quad Cities) were interested in putting on country performers.

That meant people had more opportunities to see their favorites, and that the performers commanded ever-larger fees. So festival organizers were paying more for entertainers that fewer people were coming to see. Throw in insurance costs that escalated every year, and the organizers decided to get out while they were ahead.

They were ahead. Bob Leibovitz, who assisted with the event throughout its lifetime, estimated the three non-profit organizations made about $500,000 over the course of the 21 years, or nearly $24,000 a year, which they poured back into their community-service projects.

Q: I know what "Bix" stands for in the "Bix 7" race but what is meant by the number 7?

A: It's a seven-mile run, or walk, depending on your outlook. If you do the Quick Bix, we figure it would be the Bix 2.

Of course, "the Bix" means different things to different people. If you like music better than running, it's all about the jazz festival. If you don't like running OR jazz, there's still the street festival.

Q: How does one purchase a tree and a memorial stone to be put on Ben Butterworth Parkway?

A: The memorials on Moline's riverfront park were so popular that all the spots on it basically "sold out" several years ago. However, the city has other commemorative programs.

• You can buy a brick for the Ben Butterworth Memorial "Friends of the Parkway Patio" along River Drive at 35th Street. The brick pavers are engraved with the wording of your choice.

• Commemorative brick pavers also are available for a new patio at Green Valley Sports Complex.

Each engraved brick costs $75. Call the Moline Parks Department at (309) 736-5714 for details. If you *really* want a memorial tree, they will see if there is a park with space available.

Q: Who founded AIDS Project Quad-Cities?

A: The founding members of the APQC, formerly known as the Quad-Cities AIDS Coalition, were a group of concerned citizens from several organizations. Those included the Metropolitan Community Church of the Quad-Cities, Scott County Health Department, Rock Island County

Odds & Ends

Health Department, and the American Red Cross.

To learn more, see the APQC Web site (http://www.qconline.com/apqc).

Q: What happens to all the sandbags that are used to defend against flooding after the waters recede?

A: As best we can determine, most of the sandbags go to the landfill, although the sand can be used in landscaping or for fill, according to the Rock Island County Health Department. It is not clean sand, obviously, so you wouldn't want to put it in a kid's sandbox or at the bottom of the fish tank!

Standard precautions apply. That means always thoroughly washing your hands with soap after handling sandbags or any sand or soil. (Sandbags aren't any more contaminated than the sand along any beach on the river.)

Q: With the raw sewage being put into the river during floods, are any of the fish caught out of the river edible?

A: There are no special precautions in fish consumption from the river, but keep in mind, there are some guidelines, recently issued by the state of Illinois. Carp caught in the Mississippi River near Pool 15 — north of Lock and Dam 15 in Rock Island — should be eaten no more than once a month because of chemical contamination. The same recommendation goes for channel catfish and carp from the Rock River.

Q: I recently read that the sewer plants were closing due to the floods and raw sewage will be emptied into the Mississippi River ... What does this do to our drinking water from the faucets at home?

A: Nothing. City water treatment plant operators are working harder to maintain water quality, but they say it is safe.

"We're confident we've protected the water plant from the floodwater," said Greg Swanson, Moline water-plant manager. "The challenge is to treat the floodwater and ensure its safety. We have a water-quality team on top of that and are doing extra quality control."

If you have any reason to question the quality of your drinking water (such as well water, or municipal water traveling through damaged pipes), boil it for at least two minutes or add two teaspoons of household chlorine bleach to each gallon of water before drinking it.

The bigger problem is that people who wade or must work in the contaminated floodwater are at risk for several serious illnesses, including tetanus.

Best advice: Stay out of the water. If you do get wet, make sure to wash your hands thoroughly before you eat, drink or smoke. If you are in floodwater and have a wound or cut, get medial attention immediately. You might need a tetanus shot.

Odds & Ends

Q: How much weight can the I-74 bridge hold? With all the traffic backed up it gets pretty heavy on that thing.

A: Bruce Bakke, head of Bridge Maintenance Section, Iowa Department of Transportation, said "If the question is, 'Is the bridge safe?', certainly the answer is yes. Both bridges can carry the traffic that can get on them."

Each of the two bridges has three suspension spans, a long one in the middle and a shorter on one each end. Each bridge's three spans have a combined design load of 1,300 tons, or 2,600,000 pounds, he said.

The design load is a minimum figure — each bridge could actually carry considerably more weight, he said.

The Iowa DOT does a full structural inspection of the bridges every two years. And, as those of us who use the I-74 regularly know all too well, maintenance work on the spans is done on a regular basis.

Q: I have read that the tallest structure in the world is the KTHI TV tower in North Dakota, at 629 meters (2063 feet). How close does the communications tower over near Pleasant Valley High school come to that? I'd be interested in hearing if it is taller than the Sears tower or Canada's CN tower, although I realize those are self-supporting structures.

A: The tower near Pleasant Valley High School is 1,356 feet, according to John Hegeman,

operations manager at KWQC-TV, which owns it. That's 99 feet shorter than the Sears Tower and more than 400 feet shorter than the CN Tower.

For a list of the world's highest structures, check out http://www.inquizitive.com/cgi-bin/readyref1.cgi?hid=8.

Q: How do they get the Christmas tree on top of the Kone building in downtown Moline?

A: The first tree was erected in 1966, when the elevator manufacturer's testing tower in Moline was completed. Many methods have been used over the years to hoist the tree — via helicopter and even through the tower's center. Since 1986, a crane assembled on the tower's roof assists with the tree's 18-story ascent.

The tree usually goes up early in the morning when winds are calmest. The crew swings the tree (already decorated) 180 degrees to the tower's center, where it is placed in a permanent stand. Ropes tied to the tower's corners tether the tree into place.

Q: From my house in Davenport, I frequently hear bugle calls from Arsenal Island. Is there a human playing the calls, or is it a recording?

A: The routine daily bugle calls of a military base — Reveille in the morning, Tattoo at 9:30 p.m. and Taps at 10 p.m. — are recordings,

Odds & Ends

according to Rock Island Arsenal spokesperson Vicki Stapes. Calls sounded during special ceremonies and funerals are most often played by humans, she said.

Q: How about some info on the caves and lake under Peterson Park. Any pictures?

A: The "cave" is actually an old underground limestone quarry in Moline that has been unused for many decades. The quarry, which now includes a large lake, reappeared in the public eye in 1996, when erosion uncovered a long-sealed entrance.

A number of neighborhood residents heard about the opening and explored the cavern before word got back to the property's owner, who promptly had the entrance resealed.

Sorry, but we don't have any photos of the caves or the lake. If there's someone out there who has photos to share, we'd be glad to publish them.

Q: While having drinks at a local pub recently my friend brought up a good question. How does a person consider themselves "on the wagon" when a wagon is originally the transportation of beer/alcohol?

A: It does sound a little off-base. For those who don't know, someone who is "on the wagon" abstains from alcoholic drinks, so those who "fall off the wagon" are back on the booze.

According to Chuck Moreland's *Origin of Words*, the original phrase was "on the water wagon." A water wagon was a common piece of equipment, in the days before paved roads, that was used to spray the dirt roads to help control dust.

Evidently, if you were "on the water wagon," you weren't drinking alcohol.

Q: Years ago there was a legend that if you kissed the black angel, a statue in one of the local cemeteries, you would die. I was 18 or 19 years old, foolish and fearless, so I jumped right up and French kissed that statue. I'm now 55 years old and I'm wondering when does the curse kick in?

A: We can't make any prediction on that, but for those who never heard the local legend, here goes:

The black angel was a statue at the Deere tomb in Riverside Cemetery in Moline. According to *legend*, the stone statue turned black as it stood its quiet vigil over the cemetery. Local young people used the statue as a test of bravery. The idea was to run through the cemetery at the stroke of midnight and touch the angel.

Stories abound of the luckless people who did not escape the angel's wrath. One such story is of a young man who touched the angel and died of a heart attack. Another is of a young woman who agreed to be chained to the angel overnight; when her friends found her the next day she was in a vegetative state and her hair had turned white. Stories also claim that when the angel was removed, groundskeepers called the police. The police fired several shots at the angel, claiming it was moving. The statue ended up being sunk in an unknown river where it could never hurt anyone again.

The *truth* is somewhat different. According to Gretchen Small, a historian at the Deere-Wiman House, the haunting is all urban legend.

"It's just a crazy myth, and no one ever died from it," she said.

A story in The Moline Dispatch from 1906 tells of the statue being placed in the cemetery and describes it as being "unique, beautiful, and wonderful." Ms. Small said that over the years the angel darkened due to weather, but never actually turned black. The stories of the haunting started during the late '60s. As the stories became more frequent, more and more young people visited the angel. Several cases of vandalism to the angel were reported.

The Deere family decided to take the angel down sometime in the '70s.

"It was upsetting for the family," said Ms. Small. "No one wants their family plot to be vandalized. So it was decided it would be best for the community and for the family to remove the angel."

Ms. Small said she saw a picture of the angel once, and it was beautiful. She said it had a gentle face and a long, flowing dress. One arm held a wreath and one arm was raised to the sky. She said the angel was displayed at the Deere-Wiman house after it had been removed from the cemetery, but the vandalism continued. The statue was removed and is currently being stored out of the area.

A reader adds: "During the early 1940s while the Second World War was raging, the big challenge for we people in our young teen years was to spend the night (the entire night) with the Black Angel. As I remember the wind would moan and howl in the rectangle of trees that surrounded the statue. Scary for a 13-year old."

Q: What are the names of the films that Brooke Shields made in the Quad-Cities?

A: That would be "film" — Ms. Shields starred in "An American Love," filmed here in the early '90s by the Avati Brothers, Italian filmmakers who worked here on several movies, including "Bix."

In "An American Love" she's the romantic interest in a story about an Italian literature professor on a teaching sabbatical at St. Ambrose University.

The movie was pieced together from what was originally shot as a television serial. It was something less than a smash hit.

Here's The Dispatch's review from the film's U. S. premiere, held at St. Ambrose in August of 1993:

"The premier U.S. screening of 'An American Love,' Duea Film's television serial starring Brooke Shields, took place at St. Ambrose University Saturday evening drawing capacity crowds. The movie was filmed on the St. Ambrose campus and other Quad-Cities locations during the summer of 1991.

"The line for tickets at the Galvin Fine Arts Center wound out the door. From comments in the crowd, almost everyone attending had some personal connection to the movie.

"Inside and seated, theater goers were greeted by Duea Film's producer Antonio Avati's introductory remarks. He apologized for the film's overall quality, saying it had to be transferred to video for the screening and since it was written as a television mini-series, the story would move slowly as a single viewing.

"The audience broke into laughter at the opening scenes where the camera panned the exterior and interior of a local Eagles Supermarket with Brooke doing some twilight grocery shopping.

"The early parts of the story switched back and forth from Italy to Davenport, as an Italian literature professor prepared for a teaching sabbatical at St. Ambrose. Brooke, a reporter with the campus TV station, was assigned to be his assistant.

"Other Quad-Cities scenes included Brooke jogging through an Iowa cornfield, a boat ride on the Mississippi, crossing the Centennial Bridge, an outdoor party at a Gold Coast home, a shopping expedition at SouthPark and a visit to the Buffalo Bill Museum.

"The three-hour presentation had a 15-minute intermission during which Mr. Avati and his entourage left. 'There seems to be a lot of padding of the story which is unnecessary,' said Tim Wassell, East Moline, whose wife was an extra in a bar scene.

" 'Avati was right — the sound track is bad and the pace is way too slow for a movie,' he said. Others were offended by the twangy country music sound track that played during the Iowa scenes. 'I suppose they were trying to build the ambience of the Midwest for European audiences but they made us come off as corndorks,' said Mike Hayden, East Moline.

"During the second half of the movie, the crowd broke into a groan in a cornfield scene with Ms. Shields and her Italian co-star. As they sat near a sign saying "You Can Hear the Corn Grow," Brooke mused, 'I love this land.' "

Q: **Is there anywhere I can look to see what different kind of movies were filmed right here in the Quad-Cities?**

A: We're not aware of where a filmography of Quad-Cities-made movies might be found. Perhaps someone who reads this could help.

In the meantime, trusting to memory and the Dispatch/Argus library, we came up with at least a partial list.

The movie-making heyday in the Quad-Cities came in the early 1990s, when Pupi and Antonio Avati, brothers and Italian filmmakers, shot four movies here, including one that starred Brooke Shields. Following is a list of the Avati movies:

• *Where The Night Begins*
• *Bix*
• *An American Love*
• *Brothers and Sisters*

Another non-highlight of Quad-Cities filmaking is "Beauty Queen Butcher."

Produced by Jill Rae Zurborg of Davenport and Shane Partlow of Taylor Ridge, it premiered in Davenport Feb. 23, 1992, and quickly plunged even further into obscurity than the Avati brothers' efforts.

Other films shot here include some award-winning shorts by Rob Humphrey, Jim Peterson and John Behnke, students at Augustana College in the late 1980s.

"The Yuppie," "The Real World" and "Norma Jean," films made by one or more of that trio, all picked up student achievement awards from the Academy of Motion Picture Arts and Sciences.

More recent movies filmed here include "The Law," by David Clevenger of East Moline, and "Toll Bridge to Iowa," by Augustana College student Estlin Feigley.

The movie that SHOULD have been shot here was "The Road to Perdition," which starred Tom Hanks and Paul Newman. Like most other

Odds & Ends

Quad-Citians, we were mightily disappointed that makers of the big-budget story based on the life of Rock Island gangster John Looney went elsewhere for location shots.

A reader, C.W., adds:

• "Don't forget 'Whiteboys.' Not only was some of it shot in the Q-C, but former Davenport Mayor Phil Yerington was in it."

Thanks for the reminder, C.W. Snoop Dogg makes an appearance in this story of the three white kids from Iowa who dream of being rap stars, as does Dispatch/Argus correspondent Chad Holtkamp, who was a Hollywood record executive in a cornfield dream sequence.

What other films did we miss?

• **From J.M.:** Another movie that was based in the Quad-Cities was called "Hawk Jones." It was made around '86, and starred only children!

• Hello, this is Jim Peterson of "The Trio" with a few clarifications and additions to your answer for films shot in the Quad-Cities.

Starting on the personal stuff, John, Rob and I went to Southern Illinois University. Rob and I are Rock Island natives and John is from Monmouth. We did shoot one scene of "The Real World" at Augustana, but otherwise that film was shot in Carbondale and St. Louis.

"Norma Jean" is John's short documentary of Norma Jean the Elephant who is buried in Oquawka and to whom the town has built a monument. The film aired on Showtime and The Movie Channel, but due to rights problems with Elton John's song "Candle in the Wind" used at the end of the film, it is difficult to distribute.

"The Yuppie" we shot almost entirely in the Quad-Cities in several extremely helpful local businesses. "Norma Jean" and "The Yuppie" did win awards from the Academy of Motion Picture Arts and Sciences, while "The Real World" was a finalist.

After graduating, we did a film for John Deere called "Hoofin' It" a 5 minute comedy about a man hitchhiking with his cow.

At that point, we headed to California where we wrote cartoons for Disney, Warner Bros. and other studios — some 90 episodes for 17 different series and nominated for a couple Emmys in 12 year period. We also shot an independent feature out there, but that's another story.

Recently, I moved back to the Quad-Cities to raise my children here. Our local educational system is vastly superior to Los Angeles', where I worked as an English teacher for one awful year. Since being back I have worked on some local fundraising videos for Quad-Cities institutions with Lawper Media. I am currently finishing one feature film screenplay and my next project is a script I hope to shoot here.

Enough about me, I do want to mention two other Quad-Cities area natives who are doing well in the animation business. Bill Motz, who got Rob and me into film-making back when we were all in the 3rd grade, is now a series producer with Disney and Warner Bros. Tom Hart, who some may remember as creating, writing and starring in KLJB's "Live on Tape" is also working for Disney, Warner Bros. and others.

Outside of our group, I believe Phil Dingledein and Max Collins have shot a couple of films locally, but I don't know any of the details of their productions.

Also, part of "The Blue Brothers" was going to be shot here, (at the beginning of the album Jake and Elwood are introduced as being from Rock Island, Illinois) but supposedly negotiations broke down.

Anyway, there's still a line in the film that I believe refers to the original vision of a Rock Island/Chicago cross state chase. It goes something like, "We're 200 miles from Chicago, it's dark and we're wearing sunglasses. Let's go!"

Okay, enough rambling. Thanks for the mention, keep up the good work, I read your column all the time. Thanks, Jim!

Q: Who are the Brownlie Sod House Questers 1229, and how do I contact them?

A: Brownlie Sod House Questers 1229 is an organization that maintains the Brownlie Sod House on Pine Street on the north edge of Long Grove, Iowa. The house is listed on the National Register of Historic Places. It was built in 1838 by brothers James, Alexander and William Brownlie, stonemasons who immigrated from Scotland. It's believed to be the only two-story sod house of its type in the U.S.

The soddy is open for tours at various times. Guided tours are available by calling (563) 282-4186. Admission is free. Donations are accepted. More about the house in this story is available from our files.

A reader adds: "Just a correction to the story from your files. Alexander came to Long Grove with his brothers John, James, and Robert. Ritchie was his sister-in-law, not mother. His mother, Christiana (also Mrs. Alexander Brownlie from Scotland via Canada) did come to Long Grove with some of the wives and children after their raft was frozen in the river at Alton. There are many Brownlie descendants in the Q-C area and Poweshiek Co."

Q: What are the posts for on I-280 (1 mile west of the weigh station by Coal Valley) on the south side of the interstate? They do not look like light posts and there appears to be a monitor of some sort on the cross-arm. There appears to be a satellite dish on the top portion of the vertical post.

A: Several readers sent in the same question. It's a monitoring system that weighs trucks before they get to the weigh station. If the truck checks out OK, the system signals the trucker to bypass the scales.

The company responsible for the system is called PrePass. Here's the company's explanation of its product:

"PrePass is an automatic vehicle identification (AVI) system that allows participating transponder equipped commercial vehicles to bypass designated weigh stations and port-of entry facilities. Cleared vehicles may proceed at highway speed, eliminating the need to stop. That means greater efficiency for shippers and improved safety for all highway users.

"Participating vehicles are pre-certified. Carrier's safety record and credentials are routinely verified with state & federal agencies. Prepass weigh stations employ weigh-in-motion (WIM) scales to electronically weigh the vehicles while AVI antennas verify the identity and compliance of trucks as they approach the weigh station. As a truck passes over the WIM, its axles and gross weight are calculated and the AVI integrates the PrePass transponder verifying state requirements. The AVI antenna also communicates bypass status to the driver. If weight and credentials are satisfactory a transponder green light and audible signal advise the driver to bypass the weigh station. Otherwise a red light and audible signal advise the driver to pull into the weigh station for processing."

Pretty slick, huh?

Q: **This is not a question about the cities but my husband would like to know how many gallons of water in an acre of water. Hope you can answer this. Thanks.**

A: Tell your husband: very funny. We have stated — right at the top of the main Ask Us Anything page on the Web — that we are not math people.

Nevertheless, we don't want some school kid to think that it's cool to duck a math question, so here goes:

1. *How deep is your acre? You don't specify, so we will go with enough water to cover your acre with one foot of water.*
2. *One acre-foot equals 43,560 cubic feet of water.*
3. *And, 43,560 cubic feet equals 325,851 gallons.*

Just to put it in perspective, you could take that amount of water and fill an Olympic-size swimming pool to a depth of 39 inches.

And a couple of other points of refererence:

The South Slope Wastewater Treatment Plant in Moline sends 4.5 million gallons of purified water a day back into the Rock River.

Every time a boat moves through Lock and Dam 15 at Arsenal Island, 16,330,400 gallons of water is moved.

Feel free to check our math!

Q: **I had a phone call the other day from a student asking about the traffic conditions and what I thought about having a bridge built from East Moline to Bettendorf. Are they going to build it soon or is it still in the thinking process?**

A: A Bettendorf/East Moline bridge is pretty much still in the thinking stage, though there is considerable backing for it. But no one has commited money for any of the preliminary studies that need to be done, let alone money for construction.

The Bi-State Regional Commission says initial steps must be taken soon if the bridge is to be built starting in 2020.

Q: **What happens to the ice skating surface used by the Mallards when there are other events at the Mark, like Steamwheelers football games or concerts?**

A: Nothing. It's still there, just cooling its heels, so to speak.

Seriously, the ice is covered with insulation and a temporary floor for other events.

Q: **As a kid that lives on a farm I've always been told that if you hold onto an electric fence while holding hands with someone else that they get shocked. Is there any truth to**

Odds & Ends

that? I have always been to afraid to try it.

A: We grew up on farms, too, and heard lots of things about electric fences.

"Don't touch them." was the only one we listened to. And that's all that we know on that topic.

There is a wealth of information about electric fences on the Web. We'd guide you first to this one: Farm Safety with Electric Fencing (http://www.sureguard.com.au/safetyfencing.html).

D. Nelson of Cordova adds:

Regarding the question of the electric fence, I grew up on a farm, and can assure you that if a group is holding hands, and any one of the group touches the electric fence, all will get a shock.

This took an amusing twist when our daughter leaned over the electric fence to feed the horse an apple. Our daughter was wearing tennis shoes, which insulated her from the ground … and she didn't get a shock … until the horse took the apple. The horse WASN'T wearing tennis shoes, and both got a shocking experience when the horse took the apple.

Q: How do they do the buses that are completely covered with graphics?

A: Creating what MetroLINK calls a "wrapped bus" involves a number of steps.

Images are first scanned in at an extremely high resolution and then sent on to a large format printer who specializes in exterior vinyl application. The artwork is printed on multiple sheets of vinyl and tiled onto the exterior of the bus.

Special perforated vinyl is used to cover windows, which allows passengers to see out, while people outside the bus still see the image.

Q: Wasn't there a local car dealer who was in a plane crash several years ago in north Wisconsin? Do you know the details of the crash and who it was?

A: The car dealer was Peter G. Pohlmann Sr. of Lujack's Auto Plaza. The crash was near Tomahawk, Wis., Dec. 28, 1996. Mr. Pohlmann and the nine passengers in the plane which he was piloting all survived the crash in a heavily wooded area.

Injuries to six of the 10 were so minor that they were treated and released from hospitals near the crash site. Mr. Pohlmann, the last of the remaining four to be released from a hospital, came home just three days after the wreck.

Here's a Jan. 1, 1997 story in which he described what happened:

Quad-Cities pilot released from hospital

The pilot of a plane that crashed in rural northern Wisconsin on a flight from Moline Saturday was released from Howard Young Medical Center in Woodruff, Wis., Tuesday, a hospital spokeswoman.

Peter Pohlmann Sr., president of Lujack's Northpark Auto Plaza in Davenport, was the last of 10 Iowa Quad-Cities residents aboard the Beechcraft Kingair Model C-90 to be released from Wisconsin hospitals after surviving the crash.

Meanwhile, a safety investigator said other pilots reported icing conditions at the time when the airplane went down in woods of Oneida County last weekend.

Steve Wilson of the National Transportation Safety Board office in West Chicago said his inspection of the twin-turboprop Beechcraft King-Air plane found no obvious mechanical problems.

The airplane, on a holiday trip to northern Wisconsin, crashed while on approach to the Oneida County Airport at Rhinelander.

Mr. Wilson said the plane's de-icing equipment was working properly, but there are many areas of an airplane that such equipment can't cover.

That means ice may have built up on the plane as it dropped into cloud cover at about 6,000 feet, he said.

The pilot, Mr. Pohlmann, probably had little time to maneuver the aircraft once it came out of the clouds and he could see the ground, Wilson said.

Plane passengers released earlier included Deborah S. Stafford, 48; Mary L. Pohlmann, 47; Allison L. Stafford, 16; Hugh A. Stafford Jr., 19; Peter G. Pohlmann Jr., 18; Matthew J. Forbes; 18; Amy E. Pohlmann, 23; Sarah K. Pohlmann, 21, and co-pilot Hugh A. Stafford Sr., 52. All were from Davenport or Bettendorf.

The group was headed to Conover, Wis., for a snowmobiling trip when the nine-passenger airplane landed in a heavily wooded area in Oneida County about 15 miles west of Rhinelander.

The 10 friends and relatives will forego their snowmobiling plans now, according to Mr. Stafford, who said Monday they had had enough excitement.

The group's homecoming plans were not available Tuesday. A family friend answering the Pohlmann family's telephone declined to comment. Messages left with hospital public-relations officials for Mr.

Pohlmann were not returned, and no one answered at the Stafford residence.

Mr. Stafford has credited Mr. Pohlmann's piloting ability for the group's survival.

"I think the fact that all 10 of us were able to walk out of the plane is an indication of what a great job Pete did," he said. "I think he had a little help from God, too."

"I have no question that God was there and guided me," Mr. Pohlmann said Monday, "but I had a great co-pilot, too."

Mr. Stafford said he had a number of very deep cuts in his face and lost a tooth.

"I'm all stitched up, and Pete's pretty much in the same position, although he shattered his cheekbone and he has three plates and 28 screws in his face," he said. "So he's probably the worst of the two of us, but we're in relatively good condition and good spirits."

Mr. Pohlmann was at the controls Saturday, flying through freezing drizzle, when he suddenly realized the shaking plane was going down. He said he had time to kill the engine and shove the tail down to lessen the impact before crashing.

"There was no time for fear," Mr. Stafford said.

All 10 people walked away from the plane, which was missing its tail and wings. They soon were singing songs around an impromptu campfire.

"We were able to build a fire, and we sang songs to keep everybody's spirit up," Mr. Stafford said. "Everybody was greatly relieved. We talked about how best to survive and what to do, and everyone had jobs, so they were busy and didn't think about their own problems."

The group thought they would have to camp out for the night after crashing about 11:30 a.m. However, two of the teenage victims flagged down Gar Schilling and his son, of Tomahawk, Wis., who were snowmobiling near the crash site.

Mr. Schilling returned to the road and stopped a vacationing salesman from Des Plaines and other passing snowmobilers. One of them rode to the nearest phone and dialed 911 to summon help.

Rescuers finally reached the crash site about five hours after the plane went down. Along with the human survivors, they found a pet Dalmatian named Felony, who also escaped serious injury.

The Minneapolis Air Control Center had notified the Oneida 911 Emergency Center about 11:10 a.m. when the aircraft dropped off radar screens. A Virginia air-traffic control center gave the sheriff's department last-known coordinates from the radar information about 3 p.m.

Sheriff's officials mounted a search and were within a quarter-mile of the crash site when the survivors waved down Mr. Schilling. An emergency locator device reportedly did not activate to summon rescue personnel immediately, and poor weather prevented an air search.

The cause of the crash remains under investigation. — *By Leon Lagerstam, staff writer*